Quilting Originals

Designing your own quilts

Quilting Originals

Designing your own quilts

Claire Passmore

Quilting Originals: Designing your own quilts

ISBN 978-1505890600

ISBN 1505890608

Copies of this book can also be purchased by contacting the author at her website:

www.clairepassmore.weebly.com

For Denise. This is all your fault!
I wish you had been able 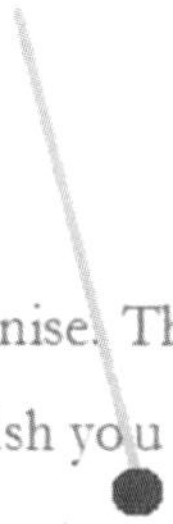
to see it. We

c

o

u

l

d

have had a

cocktail together to celebrate!

CONT

'Cape Dutch' by Claire Passmore

18 ½" x 38 ½"

Part 1

Creating an original...........1

Using this book...............3

Starting the process............5

Finding inspiration

Starting the journey

Using a sketchbook...........9

Ideas, ideas, ideas

Developing sketchbook pages

Examples of sketchbook pages

Color and value.............…...…21

How to be successful with color

Value studies

Color studies

Practical advice

From sketchbook to design..33

Design elements for quilters

Design principles for quilters

Using the Design Toolkit

Creating the design

Choosing techniques

ENTS

Part 2

The Quilts.........................49

Sardine Run.......................53

Using color and value to create luminosity and depth

eGoli – City of Gold...........…81

Balancing elements, line and texture

Bunny Chow.....................105

Telling a story with color, shapes and text

Trance Dance....................123

Conveying movement with color and line

Part 3

Dyeing your own fabric.........149

What can I dye?

What do I need?

Mixing the chemicals

Mixing the dyes

3 ways to apply dye

Resources........................167

Computer Software.......................167

Useful Websites.........................169

Supplies..............................171

Bibliography..........................173

Design Toolkit – elements...............174

Design Toolkit – principles............175

Index..........................176

'City of Roses' by Claire Passmore, 47" x 17 ½"

Acknowledgements

This book is based on journeys; the places I have been lucky enough to visit and my personal journey to becoming more imaginative and creative. I am grateful to my family and the friends who encouraged me to start this book and then pestered me until it was finished.

To my husband, Jeremy, my parents and De, Chris and Birgitta at Midsomer Quilting, thank you for your support and your belief that I could do this. Thanks also to the late Denise Tardiff, my first friend and neighbor in Cape Town, without whom I would never have begun making quilts and to Julie, who did not want to be named. Sorry, but I couldn't leave you out.

Thanks too, to the many kind and generous South Africans I have met on my travels and to you too, for taking the time to read this book. I hope it inspires you to develop your own creativity.

Part 1

I am sure, like me, you have seen many beautiful quilts at shows, in shops, books, magazines and on the internet. You look at them admiringly and think:

I'd like to make something like that, but where would I begin?

It is with this in mind that I have written this book, to share my own creative processes and explain my design decisions, step by step. I have taken this approach in the hope that I can demystify much of the jargon and theory that surrounds those ominous words 'quilt design'.

Moving away from the comfort of following a well written set of instructions complete with templates can feel like a big step. But it needn't be daunting. It is my hope that this book will build on the skills and experience you already have and guide you towards making that transition – to making your own original quilts.

As you use this book you will discover:

- ways to find and develop inspiration
- my Design Toolkit to help focus your ideas for your own designs
- straightforward methods for selecting beautiful color schemes
- guidelines to help you transform your ideas into quilt designs
- a simple, inexpensive way to make your own quilt patterns
- the benefits of experimenting with your ideas before you start
- alternative ways to use materials and to finish your quilts
- how to dye your own beautiful fabrics for your work

I hope you find this book both useful and inspiring and look forward to seeing the quilted originals you create. Feel free to contact me at my website anytime: www.clairepassmore.weebly.com

'Storm @ Cape Point' by Claire Passmore, *39 ½" x 37 ½"*

For ease of use this book has been divided into 3 parts:

- Part 1 details a variety of ways to gather ideas ready to be transformed into quilt designs. I demonstrate the use of sketchbooks as a place to develop inspiration and include suggestions and examples of methods and practical approaches that you can use for developing your own work. I have also created a Design Toolkit to provide a framework to assist the whole quilt design process.

- Part 2 contains detailed descriptions of how I used the Design Toolkit in the making of 4 quilts from my 'Destination' series. I selected these particular quilts as they show a wide variety of techniques and starting points which can be replicated in different ways. By understanding the steps I took you will see my design process in action, which can help you formalize your own ideas so that you can begin to create your own original work. From start to finish I explain the decisions I made and support this with photographs demonstrating the techniques used at each stage of the project.

- Part 3 includes detailed descriptions, recipes and photographs of the methods I use to dye fabric for my work. I include shopping lists for the basic requirements and clear instructions on how to simply and safely achieve a range of beautiful results.

Throughout the book I have included questions for you ponder. I want to stress that there are no 'right' answers, but each question is posed to give you the opportunity to clarify your thoughts or perhaps think about things in a different way.

At the end of each section you will find suggestions which I encourage you to try. These are not prescriptive lessons or tasks, but prompts to help you to develop your own creativity and give opportunities to explore your ideas further.

'Who are you looking at' *by Claire Passmore, 19 ¼" x 20"*

• Finding Inspiration

Perhaps one of the things that makes creating your own quilt designs *seem* difficult is pinpointing precisely what you want the subject of the quilt to be. Overcome this hurdle and you will unlock your creativity. It all really boils down to this: *find a starting point.*

A lifetime of experiences and emotions doubtlessly provides inspiration for our quilts, but narrowing these down and deciding how to interpret them can sometimes be challenging. Having a better understanding of ways to interpret our inspiration is definitely helpful, so you can begin to see the wood for the trees. When I first began creating my own designs this was what I found most challenging. What to choose? What should I make a quilt of? After much consideration here is my best advice:

<u>Ask yourself?</u>

What is special to me?

choose a theme

Choose something that is of special interest to you. It makes the process of developing ideas so much easier. Do you have a favorite place, color, collection, activity, person, object or photograph? Have you experienced a profound emotion that has had a big impact on your life? Perhaps you want to capture a mood or feeling. Do you want to pose yourself a question and explore possible answers? It can

be absolutely anything, but it is easier if it is something that you have strong feelings about.

My inspiration for the series of quilts illustrated in this book comes from my part-time home of South Africa. I have lived in and out of this complicated, beautiful country for several years and have fallen in love with its people and places. It has provided me with a lot of scope to develop my ideas.

This beautiful lady is busy preparing and selling food at the roadside

Having found your starting point the next step is to generate ideas. *Lots* of ideas. Many will not necessarily make good quilts, but that does not matter. This is the phase of opening up different avenues to explore. Later on you will refine them and choose one or more to develop. Time spent exploring your ideas now will pay off tenfold when you come to pinning down exactly what you are going to make.

• Starting the journey

Each great journey starts with one small step. From there on you make decisions that enable you to arrive at your destination. It is the same with making a quilt. Once you have a clear idea of your focus, you can begin to gather your thoughts and ideas and start the process that will ultimately end in your own original quilt. You may not want to plan a whole series of quilts, but to get started you need ideas, and by choosing something that you love, something that really interests you, you give yourself the best possible chance of finding the inspiration to create your own work.

Before you begin I have one further piece of advice for choosing your theme. My original choice of 'South Africa' proved to be much too broad; I needed to be more specific. So I thought about the things that I have seen and experienced that really fascinate or appeal to me. As soon as I reached *that* point my mind was quickly filled with ideas and I was able to start work. The quilts you see in this book are the results, and I have called them my 'Destination' series.

When you have your *Eureka!* moment, take the theme and let your thoughts run wild. Start recording everything you might use. I like to use a sketchbook to record my ideas. I sketch, paint, stick in pictures, tear images from magazines, add bits and pieces that I find – anything relating to my theme. I research how other artists have interpreted similar ideas and I use the internet for further sources of inspiration.

I think of how the subject makes me feel and about traditional quilt blocks that may have some link, no matter how slight. I take photographs and play about with them with photo editing software. I look through my stash of fabrics and pull out anything that seems promising and add little snippets to the page. If the sketchbook pages are too small I take a large piece of paper and use that instead. The bottom line is this – collect anything that interests you with regard to your subject, you never know what might be useful.

As time passes you will find that some ideas begin to develop more clearly than others, but once you have started you may be surprised at how quickly your pages or paper fills up.

> **Photo editing software**
>
> If you are interested in manipulating digital images there are several types of photo editing software on the market. I particularly like a program called GIMP, but this is just my personal preference. See page 167 for more details.

suggestions to try

- ✧ Identify something special to you
- ✧ Make a start on researching and recording anything about the subject that interests you
- ✧ Start to gather images, objects and ideas
- ✧ Give yourself time for ideas to develop – don't rush
- ✧ Go shopping for a sketchbook or two. Look at different types and find something you like
- ✧ Enjoy the process

Smooth Skin
Textured Barnacles

Keep the huge tail close to edge of quilt - fill all the space to show immense size

Southern Right Whale - June → October

Humpbacks - May - December

Ocean Layers of organza to give transparent look

Tail lifting known as 'Sailing' is a unique behaviour - use tail to catch the wind.

Breaching
Lobtailing
Spyhopping

Build up texture on tail with lots of thread

couch on thick thread?

Glass clear beads for water drops

Barnacle Texture

Cyamids - Whale Lice

Callosites - raised callus like patches on head

Ocean Quilting

Humpback

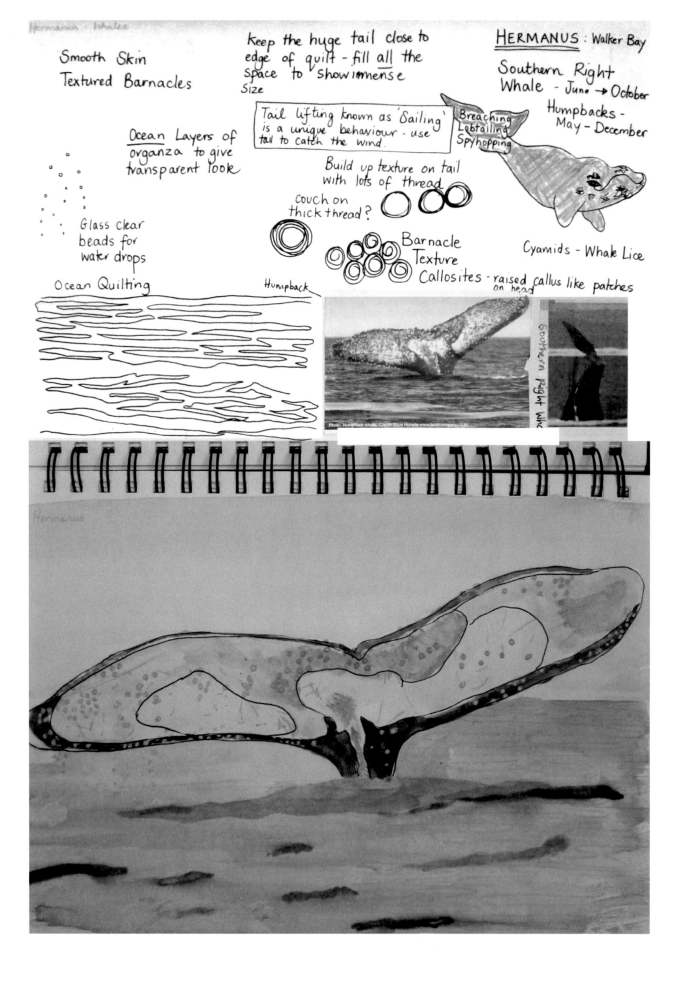

Photo: Humpback whale. Credit: Dave Hurwitz www.lazticompany.co.za

Southern Right Whale

Hermanus

No matter what you call it, scrapbook, art journal or sketchbook, it really is not important. Having somewhere to gather together your research, explorations, plans and ideas to form a growing bank of inspiration is a good idea. It does not need to be a beautiful public document; for this project, mine is a bulging, messy, mixed up book – but it does have a beauty of its own. It is a collection of drawings, collages, stitched and embellished trial pieces, experimental ideas and 'stuff' for this series of quilts, and the lovely thing is, when the quilts are finally finished, it shows the journey I have made.

sketchbook: hard cover, spiral bound with heavy weight watercolor paper

I like to keep at least one sketchbook for each of the series of quilts I make. I try to keep similar themes together but it doesn't always work out that way. Sometimes I glue or stitch pages in later or take pages out and move them, or even add fold-out page extensions if I have something too large for a single page. But how you organize it is up to you. If you thrive on order, keep it that way. If you are a more go-with-the-flow or spontaneous type of person, then have a relaxed attitude to where things end up. In this case the content takes priority over the format, so you decide.

If you do start to keep a sketchbook, and I can't emphasize strongly enough the benefits of doing so, it need not be expensive. There is a huge range available in varying sizes and formats and at different price levels. My personal preference is for inexpensive hardback books, with medium to heavy weight paper that has a bit of a tooth so that if I want to try out ideas with pastels, watercolors or other such media, the paper is ready to accept them. I also like books that have a spiral binding as the pages lie flat when the book is open, but if you want to use a double page spread you have to accept the large coil down the center. If I know I want to work across pages in this way I choose a conventionally bound book.

Sketchbook covers made from samples

For durability I prefer a hard cover as my sketchbook gets taken to all sorts of places and soft covers quickly become creased or damaged. For this reason I also like to make a cover with a tie closure to keep any loose bits and pieces safely inside. I often use fabric that has been part of experimental work early on in the design process when trying out techniques and ideas. The cover also gives added protection to the book as I carry it around – in the bottom of a bag, in the back of the car or wherever it goes.

Left: Sketchbook pages for a whale watching inspired quilt

As for size I prefer a book that gives me enough space to work on the page. For that reason I usually choose sketchbooks that measure 8.5"x 11" (or a 5" x 8" if I need a small portable book). These dimensions correspond roughly to A4 or A5 if you are more used to purchasing your paper and stationery in ISO paper sizes. But these are just my preferences. Try whatever you find, and see which size and format is best suited to your needs.

Other options for sketchbooks include recycling old books or even making your own. It can be very exciting to take an old book, paint the pages with gesso or water color and use that as a place to gather your ideas. Any text or interesting illustrations can be left to peek through adding even more richness and texture to your ideas. If you do begin to experiment with altering books and using these for your work however, be prepared to become completely absorbed by another art form. It too can be highly addictive! If you search the internet for 'altered books' I am sure, like me, you will be completely amazed and inspired by the creativity and imagination of others.

• Ideas, ideas, ideas

What goes into your sketchbook is only limited to what you can physically put in there. If it means something to you and your subject then try, whatever it takes, to include it. Photograph, squash, press, draw, paint, stick... and if you really can't get it in, keep it somewhere safe and make a note on the page so you remember where it is. For me, at this stage, it is better to include something and give yourself time to think about it, rather than discard it and decide at a later date that you wished you had kept it after all.

Expanse of the countryside
Intense Greens punctuated by
brown soil & dry grasses.

As far as the eye
can see......

Squashed wine bottle tops stuck to a page

Here is a list of some of the things I like to put into my sketchbooks. It is not exhaustive, but it gives an idea as to the type of things you can include.

Remember

You are opening up ideas at this point and it is always better to have too much rather than too little.

Don't filter things out just yet.

- drawings, scribbles and sketches
- photographs
- references to websites or books
- images torn from magazines and brochures
- labels
- color swatches made from DIY store paint card samples (see p.27)
- pressed organic matter such as leaves or flowers
- samples of fabrics, threads and materials that may be suitable
- samples from homemade print blocks
- samples of screen prints and stencils
- samples of rubbings
- watercolor, pastel, pencil, ink or crayon experiments with color and texture
- working notes and reminders
- any other bits and pieces that may be suitable

Time for a cup of rooibos tea; recycled tea bags, paint samples and sketches

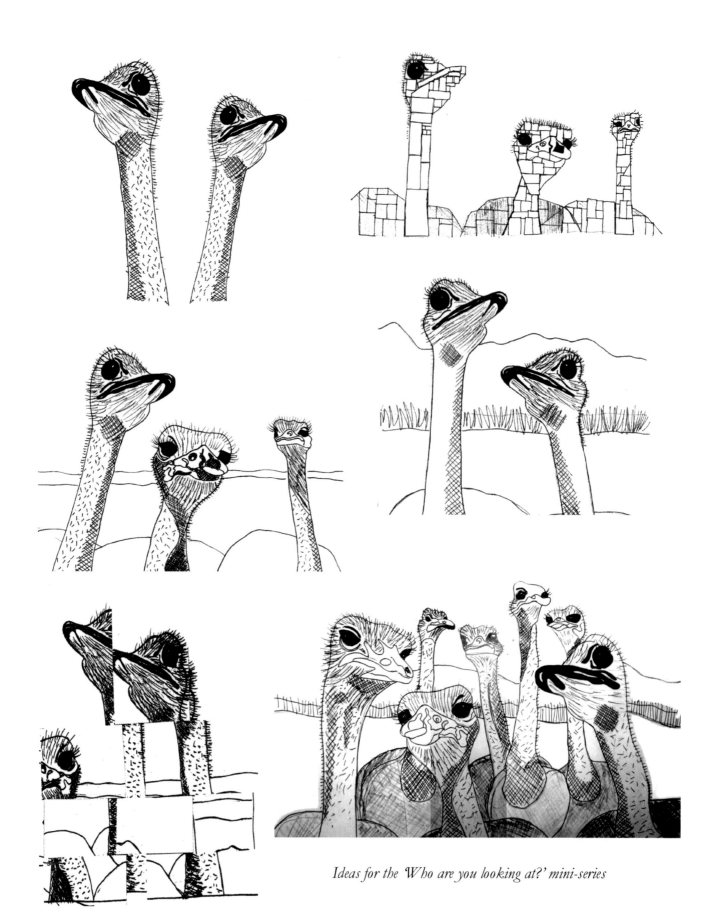

Ideas for the 'Who are you looking at?' mini-series

• Developing sketchbook pages

Sometimes my sketchbook pages resemble a scrapbook with ideas spread randomly over the page. Others are more considered compositions that are worked and re-worked until I have something that looks more like a finished quilt top. Others still, like the ostriches on the left, have drawings that I repeat in many different styles, sizes, positions and arrangements which can be transformed into a pattern for a quilt. How you use and develop your sketchbook is completely up to you, but do take the time to begin one and let your mind wander. What do you have to lose?

One important thing to remember is that a sketchbook is your place for ideas. It is not meant to be a beautiful, fully resolved piece of art in its own right – although in my opinion they do end up looking wonderful. You will have pages that are not terribly pleasing to look at, and if that bothers you, remove them or even paint or collage over them and start again. Personally I do not mind them being there – they serve as a reminder of what didn't work which is also an important part of the process.

Pages can also be altered in other ways. You can tear or cut them to different sizes, cut out windows or other shapes, stitch or glue on flaps to make pages larger or hide certain elements, add pockets or envelopes to store snippets or experimental bits and pieces… the list is as endless as your imagination.

> <u>Remember</u>
>
> A sketchbook is a place to experiment. You do not have to make it public unless you want to.

Exploring the concept of 'value' for the 'Who are you looking at?' Mini-series

(Find out more about this important concept on page 23)

WINE FARMS
Delheim
Spier
Môreson
KLEINE
ZALZE
Tokara
J.
Lourensford
WARWICK
Val de Vie
Fairview
ALLEE BLEUE
Jordan
Grape
aroma
VERGELEGEN

• **Examples of sketchbook pages**

To give you an idea of how I work, I have chosen a small collection of pages from my sketchbooks that demonstrate some different styles and approaches.

Wine Farm Pages

As inspiration for a quilt about vineyards, or wine farms as they are referred to in South Africa, I took lots of photographs at several local farms. I chose just one to make a start (see opposite). The photograph of the person at work in the vines was quite small, so I decided to extend the scene a little using watercolors and water soluble pencils to continue the vine, leaves and ground beyond the edges of the photograph. As well as forcing me to look very closely at the detail in the picture, it made me focus carefully on the colors in the scene, which will be very useful when I come to select fabrics if I develop these pages into a quilt.

As might be fitting for this subject I played about with the idea of including an image of a wine bottle. I drew the outline and filled it with the names of my favorite local wine farms. I also sketched a few grapes, copying them from a bunch I had in my fruit bowl. On the sketchbook page to the right I cut pictures of some grapes from a magazine. It is important to note that at this stage the focus is on idea generation, not being a great artist.

I thought it would also be fun to look more closely at the color of different types of wine. At a local paint store I collected a selection of paint sample cards and cut up the little sections into small chips. I used these to compare with different types of wine, matching the colors as best as I could. I then stuck them next to the names of a selection of wine types and mixed watercolors to match. These colors may also turn out to be useful in guiding me towards a color palette for the future.

Sketchbook pages for a 'Winelands'
inspired quilt

Cornflower Page

This page uses just watercolor and regular graphite pencils. In my garden I found a few dried seed pods from some cornflowers that appeared from nowhere, as a gift from Mother Nature. The page started out as drawing practice of the dried seed heads, but once they were finished I thought they looked rather lonely on the blank white page. Knowing that things often look 'right' in groups of three I drew 3 flower shapes in the space on the left of the page. They balanced the 3 tall flowers quite nicely, but looked even better when I experimented with putting each one in a box.

As the background was still just flat white I began to doodle some lines and shapes with a soft graphite pencil and wrote the name of the flower in the last remaining big space.

Using a small watercolor set I chose a very pale watery blue that was similar to the flower petals and painted both the flowers and the corner section, trying to balance the color on the page. I used a very light brown wash for the seed heads, to add some contrast and penciled in a few falling seeds for detail and interest.

I did not set out to make a planned page, but by beginning with a small drawing and then balancing some related elements around it, I organically grew the page to incorporate:

- Strong vertical elements
- A delicate blue-gray-brown color palette
- Organic shapes inspired by nature
- Interesting visual texture

It is a layout I like and I intend to explore it further someday for a series on flowers or seed heads and I think this will make a very pretty and delicate small quilt.

Gold inspired pages

These are examples of two pages where I began by writing my immediate thoughts about a chosen subject: gold. To that I added bits and pieces from magazines and tourist brochures, and scribbled a very quick sketch. As I mentioned earlier, it is one of those sets of pages that is not particularly attractive but proved invaluable in guiding me in the preparation for my quilt *'eGoli – City of Gold'*. This quilt is described in detail on pages 81 - 104. You can see that I added some notes from the trials I made with fabric and stitch – so as not to forget the settings on my sewing machine. I find that this can be a useful place to keep such information as I frequently lose odd pieces of paper with 'important' notes!

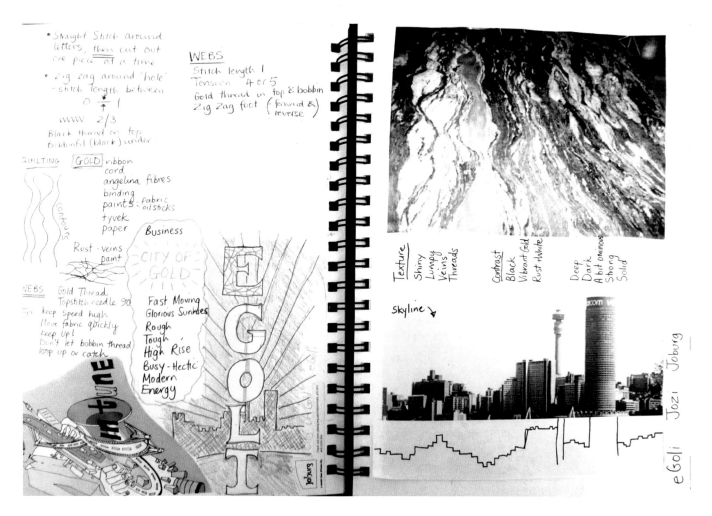

Sketchbook pages for 'eGoli – City of Gold'

Using motifs

Another different approach I sometimes use to develop ideas is to draw a simple motif and repeat it in different ways. In this case I made a page based on some ladies I saw walking along a muddy track, carrying water pots balanced perfectly on their heads. I had no camera with me, but when I got home I drew a very simple outline of a lady and she became the motif.

- by slightly altering the original motif a little I made a group of ladies walking along together
- by making the motif smaller, I transformed the lady into a child
- by adding a few background lines I put a single lady into a landscape
- by repeating the motif across the page and moving it up and down slightly I made an interesting composition
- by combining motifs together and adding some lines I created a scene with 3 people walking down the muddy track
- by repeating the single lady and painting each one in different colors using my computer I made another interesting design

Traditional quilt block inspired pages

Not forgetting the traditional beginnings of patchwork I also sometimes like to use patchwork blocks in my designs. For the quilt 'Storm @ Cape Point' I created two sketchbook pages, exploring different layouts for the well-known quilt block 'storm at sea'. Using a postcard I bought on a visit to the Cape of Good Hope I made a small watercolor painting and color study and doodled some swirling patterns that reminded me of crashing waves. There is not a lot of detail on these pages, but there was enough to give me the idea of combining traditional quilt blocks and photographic images printed onto fabric. The color study was very useful when I came to dye the fabric for the blocks and the swirling wave patterns were perfect for the free motion quilting to complete the quilt. You can see the finished quilt on page 2.

When I finally made this quilt I changed the inset image you see below from the Dias Cross to the old lighthouse. I decided to take a photograph of the old lighthouse and print it onto fabric using my home printer. It was very successful and turned a traditional block based quilt into something a little different.

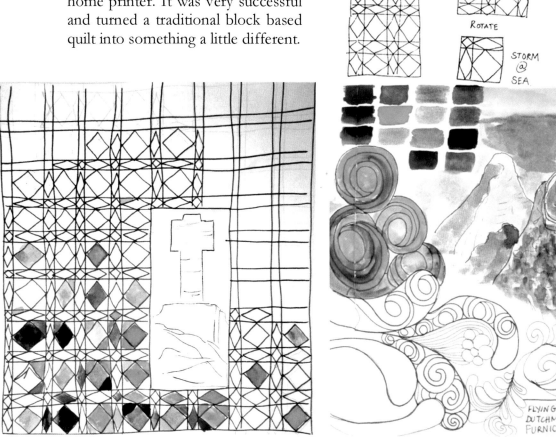

19

suggestions to try

◇ Make a few sketchbook pages - be ready to capture as many ideas as you can

◇ Don't over-think how the page looks, rather just put your thoughts onto paper and make a collection of images, sketches and doodles

◇ Use tracings, photographs and photocopies of things if you do not like to draw

◇ As one page is filled or a new idea takes shape, start a new page. Remember more is better than less at this stage

◇ Jot down notes or try out ideas with fabric or paper and find a way to add them to the page

◇ Give yourself time to play and let ideas develop

◇ Enjoy the creative process

• How to be successful with color

The whole issue of color selection is possibly one of the things quilters stress about most. Perhaps it is because there is such an enormous choice when it comes to the great variety of fabric and thread we have to work with. Whatever the reason, the important thing to know is that it is not difficult to learn about and once you have a few strategies to use, you will be able to confidently and effectively choose color palettes for your work.

I have chosen two practical and straightforward strategies to focus on which will help you develop both your understanding of color and its effective use: color studies and value studies. They are a good place to start because not only are they easy to do, but they provide useful color palettes to work from and can be used to help guide you in selecting fabrics for your quilts.

A very important factor to take into account is that color is relative and we all see and interpret it differently. I am sure we have all experienced two people discussing whether something is 'greenish blue' or 'bluish green'. The way we see color depends on many things: our cultural backgrounds, our mood, our memories, the size, shape and texture of the object, the type of light we are viewing it in and any other colors we see around it. We seldom see just one color in isolation, and the interactions between colors have a profound effect on how we physically and emotionally react to them.

From a very young age most people can name the colors they like and more often than not tend to use these first, adding a few others to make a pleasing collection. When I began to make quilts I lacked the confidence to walk into a shop and pull together a collection of fabrics. There was so much choice in terms of pattern and color that knowing where to start was daunting. Instead I relied on the shop staff to make most of the decisions for me. This was fine, and I have some lovely quilts made from other peoples' choices – but I knew that I wanted to improve my ability to select which colors to use so that the choices I made were my own. So I began reading about how artists and interior designers choose and use color and began to make sense of that huge subject known as color theory.

Ask yourself

Do I have a favourite color? Do I limit myself by tending to rely on this color too much?

21

hue the color names we commonly use

red, green, blue, yellow etc.

tint hue + white

soft and gentle; always light

tone hue + gray

can be light or dark and has a subdued feeling

shade hue + black

always dark

value the lightness or darkness of a color

this is all about comparison e.g. two types of yellow or even two colors such as yellow or blue; look at the comparative lightness or darkness

intensity the brightness or dullness of a color

is the color clean and intense or muddy and dirty?

Even though we often believe we don't know very much about color we all know a lot more than we give ourselves credit for. We know that there are literally thousands, if not more, different blues or reds in the world. We can easily compare them when they are in front of us, understanding what we see, but problems often arise because we lack the vocabulary to describe this clearly to others. For the sake of clarity I have identified 6 key color 'words' on the facing page and provided the simplest definitions I can to avoid confusion.

• Value Studies

But before getting onto color, however, let's talk value. It isn't the most exciting topic, so I'll keep it brief, but it is of great importance in turning a good quilt into a great one. Get the values wrong in your work and your quilt will be ordinary. Get them right and your quilt will sing.

Value is all about the relative lightness and darkness of colors. You can work with values in any color, but the simplest approach is to use a gray scale. If you have a graphite pencil, paint, photocopier or computer it is easy to create a strip of grays like the one below.

Grayscale

The purpose of a value study is simple. By completely doing away with the complications and distractions of color you can focus your attention on the lines and shapes in your design. Value defines those shapes, stopping them blending into each other, adding depth and drawing attention to the focal point or other points of interest you may have created.

It is said that humans can identify up to 10 different values between black and white, but practically speaking, I think that working with 3 to 5 values is completely sufficient in helping you identify what your quilt needs. Think of them as light, medium and dark, and very light and very dark if you use 5 values.

<u>Value</u>

It's all about lightness and darkness.

Value:

defines shapes

adds depth

strengthens focal points

stops a piece looking bland

helps guide the eye of the viewer

One of the more complicated aspects of designing your own quilt is dealing with the relationships between colors whilst simultaneously trying to create a great composition. By eliminating the color and creating a value study you will be able to identify what needs to be highlighted or toned down, what is coming forward in the design and what is receding and whether there is enough contrast between shapes to make them distinct

When I complete a value study I often use my computer as it is very quick and easy to render an image to grayscale. Alternatively I make a line drawing and scan it into the computer, then use the fill tool to add different values, starting with the darkest.

The 4 pictures to the left illustrate how different value combinations can change the overall look of a design.

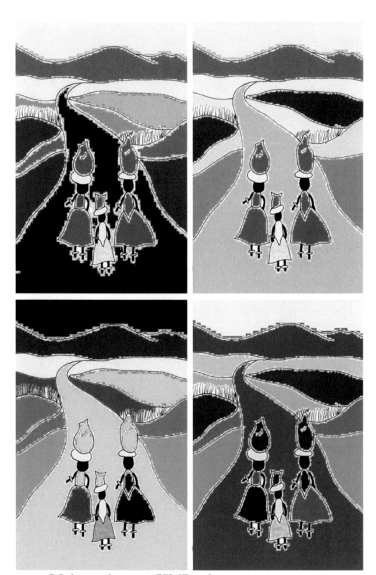

Value study using GIMP software

Ask yourself?

Do areas of the quilt or even the subject of the whole quilt guide you in your value choices?

Which combinations work well? Why?

Are there areas with too much or not enough contrast?

Do I have too few values or perhaps too many?

Are the shapes blending together too much?

What mood does the picture have? Have the value choices affected this?

I also enjoy the process of mixing paints or shading with graphite pencil. With paint you also have the option to work with a different color – but my advice is to always start with something fairly dark – perhaps a deep blue, a dark green or a burnt umber as it is easiest to create a value scale from a dark starting point. Watercolors are particularly good for this as you only need to add water to make a lighter value and by reapplying more layers of color you can achieve darker and darker values.

As you look at the pages in your sketchbook try to decide if there are certain values that you want to predominate in the design.

If nothing particular comes to mind then experiment by using different value arrangements, for the same design. The results, like the images of the ladies on the left, can be very informative.

Sometimes the mood or subject of a quilt makes the decision easy. For example, in the quilt 'Sardine Run' I used a lot of light values at the top of the quilt and gradually darkened them towards the bottom, creating a graduated effect. For this quilt the value study played a particularly important role in the overall design and was crucial in its success. You can read more about the construction of this quilt on pages 53 - 80, where I explain the development and construction of this quilt.

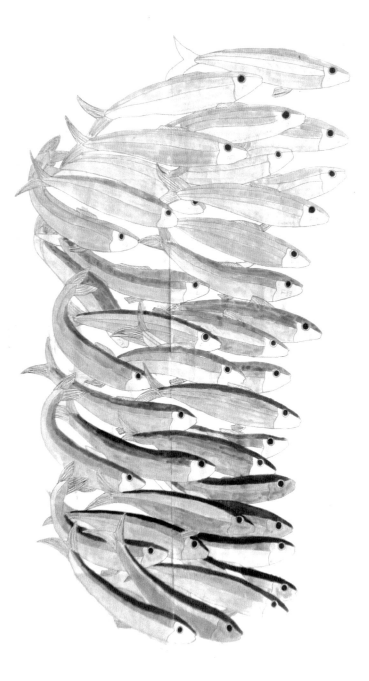

Value study with water color paints

However, this arrangement of values would not have worked well for the quilt 'eGoli – City of Gold' (see page 81) which used a lot dark values with little variation as I wanted this quilt to give the feeling of being deep underground.

• Color Studies

Ask yourself

Do I take the time to look really carefully at color?

My understanding of color and how to use it effectively has developed over time after I made a conscious decision to understand the whole subject more fully. Reading about color theory has undoubtedly helped, but I feel I have learned most from actively handling color whilst completing color studies using a wide variety of materials. The process of making color studies really helps me to focus specifically on subtle differences in hue, shade and tint which assist me in making fabric and thread choices later on in a project. One thing is certain, the more you handle and observe color, the more confident you will become when using it.

Because the inspiration for my quilts come mostly from the natural world, my life is made considerably easier as I am guided by nature with my color choices. By paying close attention to color combinations in the environment it is possible to develop an understanding of which colors work well together. Sometimes there are surprises, and colors you never dreamed of putting next to each other can look stunning.

There are many ways to approach making a color study, and I can only advise you to try out a few methods and see which you find most helpful. When I begin I always try to keep the work small, no larger than the size of my sketchbook page, and try to ignore everything except the color I see. I take an inspirational image or object and place it onto a plain background. Often that means I attach it to a clean page in my sketchbook or, if it is an object, I place it onto a blank sheet of paper. Making sure I am working in good light, I then start to look very carefully at the colors in front of me. Light and shadow make big changes in the way we see things, so pay close attention to how the color changes in different parts of a picture or on an object.

Once I have taken the time to look in detail at my subject matter I then begin to try and replicate the colors I see. This is where the fun starts. There are lots of different ways to record your observations and I am sure you will develop some methods of your own. These are some of my favorite ways.

Color study using hardware store paint samples

Next time you are at the hardware or DIY store, take a detour through the paint section and collect some of the paint sample cards they very generously give away. I use these samples to cut into small pieces or chips and try to match them as closely as possible to the source of inspiration. Once you have your collection you can sort them and play about with them, experimenting with how they look when placed in different arrangements. Store them either glued to the page or in an envelope which you can stitch or stick into your sketchbook.

As an alternative, use paints to mix your own colors and create your own paint sample cards.

Color study using technology

There are lots of different apps and software which you can use to analyze a picture you have on your phone or computer. It may be a quick photograph you take whilst you are out and about, an image you find on the internet, or even a picture you scan from a magazine or other source. One website I often use is at http://www.cssdrive.com/imagepalette/

You can also use the color picker tool from image manipulation software such as MS Paint, Photoshop or GIMP to identify the colors from your source (see page 167/168). For this photograph of a protea flower I have used the color picker tool to identify a selection of light, medium and dark values from the image. To the right of the flower I then made a swatch with the colors I identified. This swatch can be

Color study of a protea flower

taken to the fabric store to help with fabric selection for a project in the certain knowledge that the colors will look great together.

Color study using paints

Mix paint and match the colors to different parts of a source of inspiration. I like to use water colors for this purpose, but you can use any paint you have. I often use this technique when I have a picture with a lot of detail, putting small dabs of color around the edge. I try to remember to make a note which colors I have mixed, although I often forget! This method of examining color, mixing different hues together, adding gray, black and white (or water) and seeing their effects will improve your understanding of color tremendously and provides useful information should you wish to dye your own fabric. Speaking personally, this is my favorite way to make a color study.

The Bo-Kaap district in Cape Town

Color study using fabrics

As quilters, it is the fabric and thread we use that ultimately provides the color for our work. It therefore makes sense to me to use them to develop our sense of color. Gather together a nice collection of your fabrics, or go to a friendly fabric shop where they will allow you to pull out a selection of fabric to play about with. I almost always do this at the start of a project, gathering potential fabrics from my shelves and sorting them.

Begin to look at the fabrics carefully and sort them into groups. Try sorting them in different ways. For example:

according to hue –e.g. yellow-orange through red to red-purple.

according to value – e.g. from light to dark or vice versa.

tints and shades

By going through the process of sorting fabrics you will be turning the vocabulary of color into reality. It will allow you to physically compare colors so that you can more easily make sense of what you already know.

Tips

To make identifying the value of fabrics easy, sort them as best as you can then take a photo/scan or photocopy them then turn them image into grayscale on a computer. You will instantly see how much darker or lighter a fabric is compared to its neighbor.

You can also use old 3D glasses or a special tool known as a Ruby Beholder to do the same job.

Value studies are a helpful tool. Using just one hue mixed with black or white in a picture allows you to focus on composition only without the distraction of color.

suggestions to try

- ✧ Find a few nice images and objects that appeal to you
- ✧ Collect and/or make some paint sample chips and use them for color and value studies
- ✧ Try a few value and color studies with water paints and graphite pencils
- ✧ Try using a computer to identify the colors in a digital image. Change the image to grayscale and experiment with value
- ✧ Search the internet for color palette generators and try them out
- ✧ Look through your fabric collection and sort it in different ways
- ✧ Try using a Ruby Beholder or old 3D glasses and become more skilled at determining the value of different fabrics
- ✧ Try to become more aware of the color you see all around you, e.g. in shop window displays, posters, advertisements and nature

- ✧ Enjoy the process

• Practical color advice

Once you have completed a few value and color studies you will feel more confident about identifying and creating color palettes for your work. The amount of each color you use will, of course, be determined by your subject. However, when you come to using the colors you have chosen, try to vary the amount of each to achieve harmony and balance in your quilt. The following information is useful to keep in mind when making these decisions:

Value: Value is the relative lightness or darkness of one color when compared to another. For example a light blue, a mid-blue and a dark blue. Have a variety of values in your quilts to give them depth and interest (dark colors recede from the eye whilst light colors advance). When values are too similar what we are looking at seems to flatten out or blend. Value allows patchwork pieces to stand apart from one another.

Pure Hues/Colors: Using colors in their pure intense form can be very tiring on the eye, so using different values, tints, shades and tones of the same color will add interest and variety and is easier to look at. Most wide expanses of color, such as a sky, should be toned down a little so that it does not overwhelm the rest of the scene. For landscapes, in general, the larger the area you are covering the softer or less saturated the color should be.

Temperature: As you put your color scheme together, be conscious of the temperature of all the elements you are going to include. Be aware that it takes a larger quantity of cool colors, (blues, greens, purples) to cool down a hot palette, (reds, oranges and yellows) whereas it only takes a little of a hot color to warm up a cool palette.

Black, White and Gray: Look carefully at your fabrics and decide if they have a black or gray base. If they do then carefully audition them against the rest of the fabric you intend to use. Sometimes fabric with a black / gray base can look dirty or muddy when placed next to more pure colors.

Focal Point: As a very general rule, keep bright colors around the focal point or area of interest. This is one of the most powerful ways to help lead the viewer's eye to that point. It is also important that the eye has a resting place otherwise the viewer's eye jumps about without knowing where to go next.

<u>BUT...</u>

There are many so called 'rules' about color usage, but too many rules spoil creativity, and as someone famously once said,

"Rules are made to be broken."

'Big 5' by Claire Passmore, 47" x 51"

• Decision Time

The secret of designing a great quilt is to take your inspiration, make a series of informed choices, try out different options and ideas and finally refine them until you find something you love. Few people are blessed with the ability to intuitively produce great designs without working at it. I am not one of those lucky people, and secretly I think most other people aren't either. Working and reworking a design until it is just right is really important, and it takes time. When I design my quilts I probably spend as much, if not more time in the research and design phase than in actually making the quilt.

As soon as you feel you have gathered enough sketchbook material you are ready to take the next step towards creating your own original quilt. Now is the time to look carefully at the pages you have made in a new light. Which pages appeal to you most? Which pages do you think best convey the message or feeling you tried to capture? If you are not sure, ask others what they think, as they see only the sketchbook pages, not the process you went through in creating them. They will not see the things that went on inside your head as you worked, so they can objectively comment on what the images say to them.

Once you finally decide on the page or pages you wish to use, take a moment to congratulate yourself as now you begin the process of developing your original design. It is a process that needs you to make lots of choices, but do not worry - you can always change your mind, so don't shy away from making decisions.

To help make these choices there are numerous widely accepted guidelines that artists and designers use, known as the principles and elements of design. When I first started designing my own quilts I focused a lot of my attention on these guidelines and I can honestly say I felt overwhelmed by them. They are not necessarily complicated, but there are a lot of them and they include many variations and options. To try to make sense of it all I decided to approach the design process in a systematic way, and created a Design Toolkit which brings relevant design principles and elements together in one place. Really it is just a way of breaking the elements and principles into small manageable pieces and as I have become more confident and familiar with them I rely less on the Design Toolkit to structure my ideas because the

Ask yourself

What is the meaning I want to convey with this quilt? Have I conveyed what I was trying to capture?

Ask yourself

Do I like making decisions?

Yes? - Great! I am going to find this easy.

No? - Don't worry; I have a Design Toolkit that will help until you become more confident. Read on!

guidelines it identifies have become embedded into my mind. As you practice your own designing skills I am sure you too will see this change. At the start, however, I found the toolkit approach helpful and I will demonstrate how I used it later in this chapter so that you can try using it should you wish.

Firstly, however, I will briefly outline the elements and principles of design in relation to quilting.

• Design elements for quilters

Design
Elements

Line

Shape

Color

Texture

Space

In 'design-speak' the lines, shapes, colors, textures and arrangements of images you have put into your sketchbook pages are referred to as design elements. Some of these will eventually become the seams, fabric pieces, appliqués and stitch lines on your finished quilt. As a quilter they are what you work with. On page 39 you will see an example of how I take these design elements, and use the Design Toolkit to isolate elements from a sketchbook page so that I can decide what to do with them next.

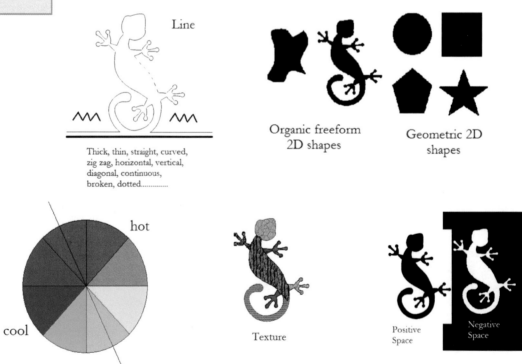

Line

Thick, thin, straight, curved, zig zag, horizontal, vertical, diagonal, continuous, broken, dotted..............

Organic freeform 2D shapes

Geometric 2D shapes

hot

cool

Texture

Positive Space

Negative Space

• Design Principles for quilters

Design principles are simply guidelines that help you decide how and where you place those elements I have just outlined in your design, adding to its impact and making it all the more pleasing and interesting to the eye. In other words *how* you arrange those lines, shapes, colors and spaces that you have already put in your sketchbook. Knowing the principles and selectively applying them can not only be helpful when you are developing your design, but also when you can't figure out why a design is not working. As you become more familiar with the principles you will see that a lot of it is just common sense that you already know, but possibly had never really analyzed before.

I have one word of caution, however; know about them and use them, but do not let them get in the way of your own creativity. *This is art after all!*

Balance: the elements in your design can be visually balanced on the quilt top in several ways:

Design Principles

Balance

Harmony

Contrast

Dominance

Rhythm

Unity

- *symmetrical:* evenly balanced either side of a line; think of a mirror.
- *Radial:* evenly spaced around a central point – but not necessarily central to the whole quilt; think of a wreath.
- *asymmetrical:* a large shape close to the center of a quilt can be balanced by one or more smaller shapes closer to the edge; think of a child's seesaw. In a similar way, a large dull shape can be balanced by a small bright one elsewhere.
- *Mosaic:* where shapes are spread equally over the surface and no single one has dominance; think of the balanced chaos of an all-over pattern.

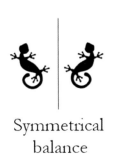

Symmetrical balance

Radial balance

Asymmetrical balance

Mosaic balance

Having many of your design elements on one part of a quilt and little or nothing on the rest will look unbalanced. Unless you especially want the composition to appear this way then it will be necessary to try to balance the elements more effectively.

Harmony

Contrast and dominance

Harmony: this is the pleasing co-existence of all the elements in a design. It can be achieved by combining similar, related elements together. Grouping similar shapes, textures, quilting designs, or adjacent colors on the color wheel are good examples. Repetition of shapes is also harmonious, giving a uniform relationship between them. Another way to harmonize designs is to allow seam or quilting lines to intersect or guide the eye, joining elements or making connections between them. This helps the viewer to make sense of what they are looking at and interpret what they see.

Contrast and Dominance: at the opposite end of the spectrum from harmony, contrast and dominance differentiate the elements you use. A quilt without just a little variation can be rather boring and look very regimented or predictable. Making changes to the angle, size or color of one or more shapes, can add some variation and give one (or more) elements more importance or impact over others.

Compare the two collections of geckos on this page; I used the same layout but made the center gecko red in the bottom one - this interest breaks up what could otherwise be a rather monotonous composition. Other ways to achieve this could be by using a larger square in a group of smaller squares or using a single circle in a group of squares. Alternatively using one or more green shapes amongst a group of blue shapes would also provide contrast and perhaps single it out for special attention.

36

Rhythm: is about predictability and order. As an example, day and night are probably the most predictable pattern we know. Rhythm is a word we are familiar with in a musical sense and when it is lacking or absent we change its name and call it noise, but when it is organized at regular intervals, it becomes pleasant to the ears. In a similar way rhythm in design becomes pleasing to the eyes. Rhythm can be achieved by placing elements so that they follow a regularly pattern or path, or at regular or predictable intervals. It has to do with the placement of elements relative to each other. Here are some suggestions.

Rhythm

Circular – going around in a circle, or radiating from a point

Spiral – moving out from a point

Linear – horizontal, vertical, diagonal or combinations

Arranged in a geometric shape – e.g. circular, triangular, square

Arranged in recognizable shapes – such as C, L, S, T, U, Z

Grids – in a regular grid pattern

Symmetrical or Asymmetrical

Often the layout you use can be related to the subject matter you have chosen, although there is no special reason for this to be so. My quilt 'Trance Dance' (page 123), has a spiral / circular structure which I used to specifically emphasize the movement of the figures in the scene. In contrast, the quilt 'eGoli – City of Gold' (page 81) has a strong vertical structure with quilting lines radiating from the central column. I chose the strong vertical as I wanted to emphasize the idea of the gold being deep beneath the ground, and the radial quilting lines focus the viewer's attention inwards to the city skyline.

Unity: it is interesting to note that the principle of harmony seems to directly contradict those of contrast and dominance. The art of balancing this sameness and difference at the same time is called unity. Unity is the overall arrangement of all the elements you use in a regular and consistent manner so they complement each other and work in unison, allowing everything to fall into place. To sum up, when all the given principles of design work in perfect synchronization, unity is achieved. If anything looks out of place or 'does not belong', then unity has not been achieved.

> **Ask yourself**
>
> How do I want to organize the elements in my design? Does the quilt subject guide me or do I have free rein?

• Using the Design Toolkit

As I mentioned earlier, using the Design Toolkit helped me a lot in the early stages of my journey into quilt design. I knew about the elements and principles of design, but found it all kept swimming around in my head whilst I was trying to think about how I wanted my quilt to look. With the prompts in front of me I was able to look at my sketchbook pages more clearly, isolating the things I wanted to include in the quilt clearly in my mind. I was then able to understand how I could change them or position them to the best effect. I want to stress that I am not advocating a 'one size fits all' approach for designing a quilt, but it was a helpful place to start when I was getting to grips with everything. If this appeals to you, then please give it a try, you will find blank copies of the Design Toolkit on pages 174 and 175 which you are free to photocopy for your own use. I found that by the time I had finished working through the prompts I was clear in my own mind as to what I was going to focus on and how I might go about proceeding to the next stage.

The following description is a generalized example of the process I go through each time I design a quilt from scratch using sketchbook pages. Much of it goes on quickly inside my head, but for the purposes of clarity I have completed a Design Toolkit with the kinds of questions I ask myself whilst looking at my sketchbook pages. At every step along the way I ask myself *what* and *why*? What shall I put here? Why am I choosing this? Why am I putting it here? Why does this look 'right'? Usually the answer lays in the principles of design. By training yourself to notice these things you will find the design process becomes easier. We take so much for granted when we see things because it is 'just the way they are', but by noticing the *what and why* we can start to use them more effectively in our designs, making it a conscious process rather than just guesswork.

As you start your quilt design, if it has not already become clear, now is the time to specifically identify the meaning you want the quilt to convey in just a few words. For 'Sardine Run' I wanted people to see *a swirling shoal of fish in a luminous ocean*. For 'eGoli' I wanted to show *a city that grew from gold, deep under the ground*. Next I begin focusing on the elements of the design I want to include and once I have established these I move on to the principles.

Design Toolkit© for Quilters: elements

www.clairepassmore.weebly.com

Lines	Shapes	Space	Colors	Textures
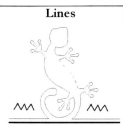	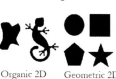 Organic 2D shapes Geometric 2D shapes	 Positive Space Negative Space	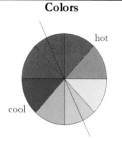 hot cool	 Texture
Thick, thin, straight, curved, zig zag, horizontal, vertical, diagonal, continuous, broken, dotted............ Pay attention to why you drew the lines and what they might be emphasizing	2 dimensional flat shapes are made from lines which have been joined up They are either organic or geometric	The area around, within or between shapes or parts of shapes Important for perspective Can be positive or negative	Hues, Shades, Tints, Tones, Values Color and Value studies help with this element	Can be physical or visual, real or implied Makes use of threads, different fabrics and patterns or prints

What kind of lines did I draw? Wiggles/spirals /zig zag /straight /curved /angular / patterns /doodles....
How did I draw the lines? Are they thick/ thin/ heavy/ feint/ solid/ dotted/ smooth/ erratic/ scribbled/crisscrossed.............
Do the lines suggest something, such as sparkles, vibrations, movement?
Do the lines form a structure or perhaps divide things apart?
Do the lines join up to form shapes or are they just isolated lines?

What are the shapes I am looking at?
Are they regular or irregular?
Are they isolated shapes or do they fit together in some way?
Do they fit together to form a bigger shape?
Do they overlap each other?
Do they do something else? If so, what?
How much visual weight does each of the shapes have?

Did I use the space on the sketchbook page in a special way to show an idea?
Look at the areas around, within and between the shapes. Is their position important? Does it help tell the story of the page?
If not, do any words come to mind about the subject that will help? Deepness, separateness, wide open space, closeness, partly hidden, intimate, cosy, regimented, ordered, rows, lines, diagonals, overlapping, perspective, positive space, negative space..........

Does the subject on my page(s) guide me towards a certain color scheme? Perhaps hot or cold, natural, light or dark, shocking?
Would a color study guide me towards a palette of colors for my quilt?

Is there obvious texture I want to include in the design?
Do any words spring to mind with regard to the subject?
For example: airy, bristly, bumpy, coarse, dimpled, feathery, filmy, fluffy, fuzzy, gaseous, glassy, grainy, greasy, gritty, hairy, hard, leathery, lumpy, matte, metallic, moist, mushy, oily, powdery, prickly, resilient, rough, rubbery, sandy, sharp, silky, slick, slippery, smooth, soft, spongy, velvety, wet, wooden
Are there shadows which change the texture in some parts?
How could I portray these textures?

Design Toolkit© for Quilters - principles
(Toolkit for placing design elements)
www.clairepassmore.weebly.com

Harmony	Contrast and Dominance	Rhythm	Balance	Unity
				Overall arrangement of lines, shapes, colors and/or textures complement each other
Repeated lines, shapes, patterns, colors, motifs or textures Gives calmness and is easy on the eye Too much can be boring	Variation of lines, shapes, colors, textures, orientation Think of opposites, e.g. light and dark Gives importance, impact & variation	Predictable and organized order of lines, shapes, patterns textures colors or motifs Can be regular, progressive, alternating or flowing Helps guide the eye	Elements arranged so that visual weight is balanced: symmetrical, radial, asymmetrical, mosaic, big balanced by many small, or small bright shape balanced by larger dull shape	Nothing appears out of place and there is consistency within the design Grouping and/or repeating elements contributes to unity as does continuing lines, shapes, colors, textures or techniques throughout the design

Do I have a clear idea of what my quilt is going to be about by now?
What is the meaning / story I want to convey?

Which elements from my pages will I use?
Do I want some to be more important than the others?
How will I show this? Size, color, position, isolation...

Do I want all elements to be equal?
Will this make my quilt look boring? How will I stop this?

Do I want to repeat any of the shapes, lines, textures or colors?
Which ones? How often? Do I have enough, or perhaps too many?
Should they be exactly the same or slightly different in some way?

> Try drawing or tracing the shapes and cut them out.
>
> Physically move them about on the page or computer screen.
>
> Give yourself time to play.

Is there going to be a pattern to any repeated elements?
Do I want to create an organized or chaotic pattern from these repeated elements?
How can I lay them out? Circular, spiral, triangular, square linear, letter shaped pathways e.g. S, C, Z.... grid like, rows, columns, scattered, densely packed, overlapping......

How will I balance them?
Are there spaces that are too full or too empty?

So far, does everything complement this idea? Does everything 'belong'?
Are the shapes, colors style all working together or is there an 'odd man out'?

Can I piece these shapes or use applique or thread?
Will the lines be seams, strips or stitches?

• Creating the Design

Once I have analyzed my sketchbook pages I am finally ready to create the design. The Design Toolkit has given me the framework, now I need to settle down and start to experiment with the lines and shapes I have identified, tracing, scanning, photocopying or redrawing them from the sketchbook pages. I make copies of these drawings and enlarge or reduce them in size as indicated by the decisions I made with the Design Toolkit. Using paper, scissors, glue and my camera I try out different ideas and layouts, moving things around on the page, making copies or taking photographs as I work. This allows me to compare different layouts directly and helps me make better decisions. The Design Toolkit helps to remind me of the things I wanted to try and if those ideas do not work I return to it for fresh ideas.

As another alternative you can also use a computer to manipulate images and try out different ideas. Image manipulation software such as GIMP gives the possibility to easily create lots of different options and then compare them until you find the ones you like most.

Once I find the final arrangement of all the elements I want in my quilt I decide whether I need to make a pattern. If I do, I usually draw it by hand and then enlarge it to the full size of the quilt, but I do also use the software from Electric Quilt from time to time ('Storm @ Cape Point' on page 2 is an example) and image manipulation software such as GIMP. I find using a computer to manipulate images a very useful tool, especially when enlarging or reducing them. I particularly like the freely distributed software called PosteRazor which allows you to very simply change the size of any image you have scanned then save it as a PDF file which you can print. It saves a fortune in photocopying costs, and allows you to experiment with resizing by percentage, the number of pages or absolute measurements (imperial or metric) at home. Details of the software I like to use can be found on pages 167 and 168.

Although I call this the 'pattern' for the quilt it does not mean the design process is over once the pattern is drawn. The design is still a work in progress, and I often make changes as I work, but it is this final drawing that I enlarge to the full size of the finished quilt, creating a pattern that I can cut up and use.

Tip

Tracing images can be particularly helpful, since the transparency of the paper allows you to experiment with overlaying and overlapping images to help decide their placement.

Tip

Enlarge or reduce picture or drawing dimensions on your computer using software such as PosteRazor.

You can then print them out on your home printer at full size and stick the pages together to create patterns of any size.

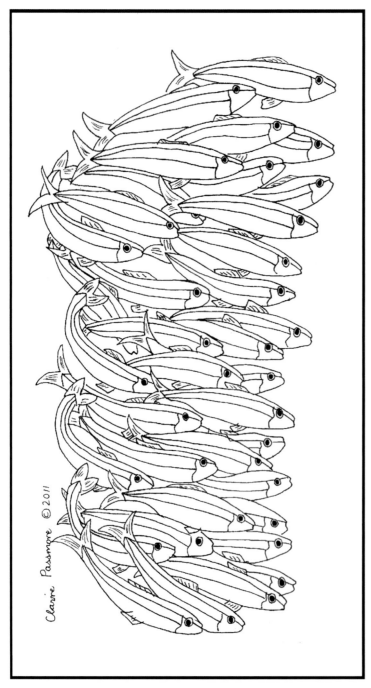

Pattern for 'Sardine Run'

Pattern for 'Who Are You Looking At?'

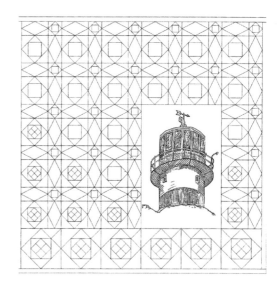

Pattern for 'Storm @ Cape Point' made using Electric Quilt (EQ7) software

42

• Choosing Techniques

When my pattern is ready I begin planning to transform it into the finished quilt. I think of the design in terms of the layers which will finally be merged together:

background   *foreground*   *quilting*

As these are the layers quilters work with when using fabric and thread, now is a good time to begin to consider the techniques you might use to create these layers. Do you love appliqué, or do you avoid it if you can? Do you prefer to piece fabric by hand or by machine? Do you sew curves with ease? Are you more comfortable when you can cut and measure, or are you happiest when you just cut and sew and see what happens? Will paint or thread sketching give you texture and the effects you desire? You need to analyze what you love to do and then think about whether you want to branch out gently and try something new, or push yourself to try something completely different. When you are clear in your own mind about what you like and what you are good at you can then think about developing your skills to try new things.

Ask yourself?

Which techniques do I use often? Do I want to try something new?

When designing my quilts I draw on all my past quilting experiences – traditional, contemporary and experimental. Some of my quilts are more traditional in their appearance, using tried and tested blocks and techniques, often mixed with more improvised methods. Others are more contemporary and use a variety of materials that make life simpler or add different effects to fabrics. What I like to do best, however, is to experiment. My mind is constantly thinking *what if?* Because of this my quilts often evolve as they are made. My starting point is just that – somewhere to begin. What I plan to make at the start, and how the quilt finally turns out can sometimes be quite different. But that is what I find exciting and I have stopped worrying about it!

I find it helpful to ask myself the questions on the following page as I ponder my next steps. They help me organize my plan of attack. They give me a new focus from which I can build my ideas for the quilt I ultimately want to make.

Ask yourself

- Do I have some sketchbook pages ready to turn into a quilt?
- Do I have a clear idea of what I want this quilt to portray?
- Have I given myself enough time to play with my ideas?
- Am I ready to try the Design Toolkit?
- Do I want to use pencil and paper, a computer or other tools to help with the design process?
- Which materials could I use?
- Do I already have them or do I need to make or purchase any further materials?
- Which techniques could I use?
- Do I need to research or learn a new technique?
- Do I need to start experimenting to achieve a certain 'look'?
- Is there something new I would like to try?
- Is there something too difficult to translate with fabric? If so, how else could I make it work?

Trying out different quilting patterns

suggestions to try

✧ Look through your sketchbook and choose a few pages to work on

✧ Identify some design elements

✧ Manipulate the shapes and images in different ways

✧ Experiment with different layouts to see how the changes can alter the look of the some of your designs

✧ Make a value study for some of your favourite designs

✧ Draw or print out a final drawing of how you think the quilt will look. Try using software such as PosteRazor to enlarge it to a 'pattern' size

✧ Choose a color palette for your work

✧ Think about the techniques you can use to transform your pattern into a quilt

✧ Try something new

✧ Don't rush the process. Take time to experiment and try out as many options as you can. It is time well spent

✧ Enjoy the process

'Greetings From the Rainbow Nation' by Claire Passmore, 40" x 39"

Part 2

20° 00' E

The Quilts

34° 50' S

Here in part two I describe in detail the entire process of creating four of the quilts from my 'Destination' series. Starting from a blank sketchbook page through to the finished quilts I explain the thought processes and decisions I made as each quilt took shape. I have tried to be as detailed as possible so that you can see the steps I took and begin to formulate your own ideas and approaches to designing and making your own original quilts.

I have deliberately not done this for every quilt in the series as it would have led to unnecessary repetition. Instead I have selected the quilts that demonstrate a variety of approaches and techniques I like to use. You are free to make your own version of these quilts if you wish, although that would rather seem to defeat the aims of this book. Instead, I hope to inspire you towards creating your own original designs.

Left: *'Where Two Oceans Meet' by Claire Passmore,* *13" x 31"*

Sardine Run	
Inspiration	An event
Pattern	Hand drawn
Color Study	Water colors
Techniques	Raw edge appliqué
	Machine trapunto
	Hand dyed fabrics
	Layering of sheer fabrics
	Machine quilting
Finishing	Raw edges

eGoli - City of Gold	
Inspiration	A city
Pattern	Letter stencil and city outline
Color Study	Paint chips
Techniques	Cutwork
	Machine needlelace
	Hand dyed fabric
	Painted fusible web
Finishing	Traditional binding and satin stitch

Bunny Chow	
Inspiration	A meal
Pattern	Hand drawn
Color Study	Mood colors
Techniques	Raw edge appliqué
	Machine trapunto
	Layering of sheer fabrics
	Machine quilted writing
Finishing	Corded edge
	Custom made hanger

Trance Dance	
Inspiration	An original art work
Pattern	Hand drawn
Color Study	Paint chips
Techniques	Raw edge appliqué
	Stenciling
	Curved piecing
	Hand dyed fabric
	Hand stitching
	Machine quilting
Finishing	Traditional binding

'Long Walk to Freedom' by Claire Passmore

'Sardine Run' by Claire Passmore, *27 ½" x 44"*

Techniques

Raw edge appliqué collage

Machine trapunto

Fabric dying

Layering sheer fabrics

Free motion quilting

Design Focus

Using color and value to create luminosity and depth

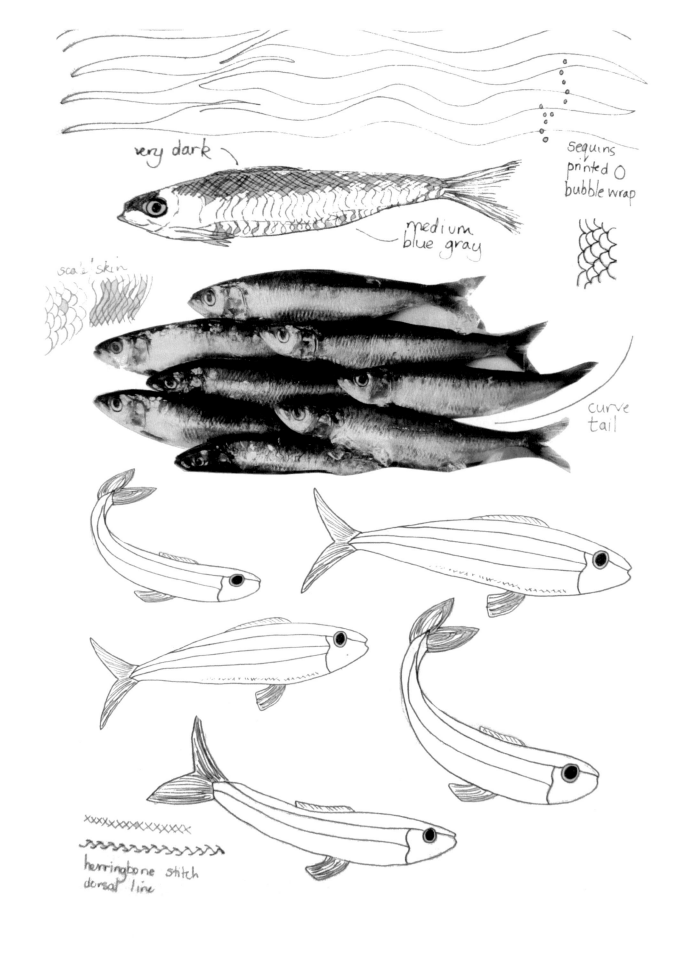

very dark

sequins
printed O
bubble wrap

medium
blue gray

scale skin

curve
tail

xxxxxxxxxxxxxxxx

herringbone stitch
dorsal line

• The Greatest Shoal on Earth

Called 'The Greatest Shoal on Earth' by the BBC, the Sardine Run is a little understood phenomenon. It occurs most years off the coast of South Africa, sometime between the last two weeks in May and the first two weeks in June. Literally millions of sardines form enormous shoals and are rounded up by the cold water current that flows up the South African Coast towards Mozambique. Predatory sharks, seals, dolphins, gannets, cormorants, gulls and many other species take advantage of the amazing quantity of easy food, the result being a feeding frenzy of enormous proportion. It seems that dolphins are primarily responsible for rounding up huge numbers of sardines into huge swirling bait balls which twist and turn in a huge mass, as individual fish attempt to avoid being eaten. The sardines usually appear between Port Elizabeth and Port St Johns, so if you wish to witness the spectacle these are the towns to aim for.

There are sardines down there somewhere!

• Sketchbook Inspiration

This quilt was the first in this series. From the first day I arrived in South Africa I had heard people talking about the phenomenon of the Sardine Run and having never seen anything like it before I was curious to find out more. So I decided to set off on a trip to Port Elizabeth in search of the small silver fish. What I had not counted on was the difficulty of capturing it on film. The huge schools of fish form and break up very quickly, literally popping up and disappearing within minutes. I discovered quite quickly that the most reliable way to spot one is to look up rather than down, searching the sky for the telltale sight of diving gannets, but inevitably I always arrived too late.

The closest I got to seeing a sardine was in the local supermarket! So much for the romantic idea of finding my own images that I could use. Fortunately all was not lost. Thanks to the incredible National Geographic TV Channel I have been able to see even better images of the Sardine Run than I could have ever hoped to capture myself and it is these images along with some real sardines that were my references for the quilt.

Left: A simple sketchbook page

Picture courtesy of TANAKA Juuyoh (田中十洋) Wikimedia Commons

As I watched this incredible spectacle there were two main things that struck me: the first was the speed at which the fish and their predators move, and the second, the deep color of the ocean and the silver fish. The blue of the water is intense, and the flashes of silver as the fish change direction in their efforts to escape the jaws and beaks of their predators is incredible. These are the things I wanted to capture in my quilt.

Super (market) sardines

With no photographic images of my own to refer to I turned to something even better; the real thing. From a local supermarket I bought some fresh sardines and made some simple outline drawings of the fish. (I ate them afterward – I hate waste!) I also used them for a color study using watercolors, recording the variety of colors on their silvery bodies. As you can see to the right, the range of colors was very subtle and gave a pale, virtually monochromatic palette.

Using the inspiration I had gathered in my sketchbook and the general ideas I had for the quilt I decided to try using my newly created Design Toolkit for the first time, in order to try to formalize my thoughts for the design.

Color study using watercolors

• Using the Design Toolkit

Design Toolkit© for Quilters - elements

www.clairepassmore.weebly.com

Lines	Shapes	Space	Colors	Textures
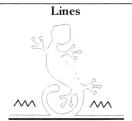			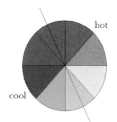	
Thick, thin, straight, curved, zig zag, horizontal, vertical, diagonal, continuous, broken, dotted............	Organic freeform 2D shapes Geometric 2D shapes	Positive Space Negative Space	hot cool	Texture
Pay attention to why you drew the lines and what they might be showing	2 dimensional flat shapes are made from lines which have been joined up They are either geometric or organic	The area around, within or between shapes or parts of shapes Important for perspective Can be positive or negative	Hues, Shades, Tints, Tones, Values Color and Value studies help with this element	Can be physical or visual, real or implied Makes use of threads, different fabrics and patterns or prints

Smooth lines to suggest calm water – horizontal, gentle

Smooth curved lines of fish shapes
Regular smooth bumps for fish scale pattern

Many repeated simplified fish motif shapes - almost identical

The fish need to be closely packed & overlapping - to create a
dense mass.   No single fish should stand out from the rest
The 'ball' of fish to be surrounded by lots of open blue water/space

Luminoscity – how to achieve this???
Impression of depth of water – how to achieve this???

Try transparent fabric layers – organza, tulle, net, Angelina fibres, metallic and rayon threads
Light values near the surface/top of the quilt ⎤
Values gradually darken towards the bottom.   ⎬ Will need careful grading.
Grading the values of the water and fish   ⎟
Color and value study based on real fish   ⎦

Overlap the fish to create 3D effect

Palette to be mostly blue and gray based. Very cool and calm

Texture needs to be kept smooth too – threads need to blend rather than contrast

Design Toolkit© for Quilters - principles
(Toolkit for placing design elements)
www.clairepassmore.weebly.com

Harmony	Contrast and Dominance	Rhythm	Balance	Unity
				Overall arrangement of lines, shapes, colors and/or textures complement each other Nothing appears out of place and there is consistency within the design Grouping and/or repeating elements contributes to unity as does continuing lines, shapes, colors, textures or techniques throughout the design
Repeated lines, shapes, patterns, colors, motifs or textures Gives calmness and is easy on the eye. Too much can be boring	Variation of lines, shapes, colors, textures, orientation….. Think of opposites, e.g. light and dark. Gives importance, impact & variation	Predictable and organized order of lines, shapes, patterns textures colors or motifs Can be regular, progressive, alternating or flowing Helps guide the eye	Elements are arranged so that visual weight is balanced; symmetrical, radial, asymmetrical, mosaic, big balanced by many small, or small bright shape balanced by larger dull shape	

Create an impression of a ball of moving fish swimming closely together on a semi-luminous blue background
Repeated motif of the simple fish shape in a variety of 'poses'…
angled / slightly curved / slight variations in size
No single fish to stand out from the rest

Need to use lots of different but closely matched fabrics to make the fish similar but interesting

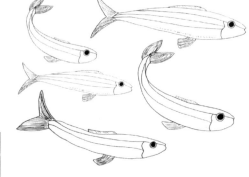

Use commercial print fabric to take advantage of differences in color and pattern
Maybe over dye some of the fabrics to marry the colors more???

Use detail of quilting to create visual texture on fish bodies and water to make people want to take a closer look. Try using trapunto technique to make fish physically stand proud of the quilt surface. Quilt the background densely to flatten and smooth it and make the fish stand out even further

Make use of quilting lines for water and scales; take advantage of natural rhythm of the pattern in these elements

Keep the densely packed fish motifs in a central ball/column – all swimming in the same direction.
Overlap almost every fish to create the illusion of depth of field
Use value to create the illusion of depth of water – light top to dark bottom

Keep a large area of blank space around the mass of fish
Put the calm wavy quilting lines here for contrast and quilt densely to give smooth water feeling
Maybe try piecing the fish to try something new

• Developing the Design

Looking at the notes I made on the Design Toolkit pages I was able to clearly see both what I wanted to include on the quilt and how I could achieve my goal of creating a shoal of sardines from fabric. I was very pleased that I had finally been able to make sense of the principles and elements of design that had overwhelmed me in the past, and the best thing of all was that I now had a clear image in my mind's eye of how I wanted the finished quilt to look.

I began creating the design by constructing the shoal of fish. I knew I would need to draw fish in a variety of positions and a variety of sizes, so I watched the National Geographic Channel clips many, many times, pausing the picture often, trying to find images to draw. Unfortunately, I quickly discovered the fish move so quickly that it was virtually impossible to see them move in anything other than straight lines and so was of no use in this respect. I needed to find a better solution, so I decided to look again at some real fish. To capture their sleek outline and movement on paper I manipulated and twisted them slightly, drawing simple outlines of what I saw. As I examined the fish I also noticed how their coloration was separated into bands; a very dark section along the top of the body, transforming into a bright, light reflective silver band through the central dorsal line. This then became a blue gray color towards the fish's belly, suggesting I should divide the fish outlines into 3 or 4 sections.

I began by drawing 3 very simple fish, adding just a little 'bend' to give them the feeling of movement. Using the ideas I pulled together with the Design Toolkit, I identified that I wanted to have the numerous fish in different sizes and positions to add interest and perspective to the shoal. Rather than draw thirty or so individual fish I realized that all I needed to do was re-size these 3 drawings using my favorite PosteRazor software (see page 168) and then make minor alterations to the fish, should it be necessary.

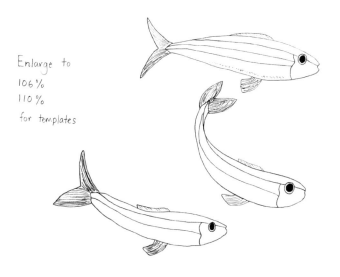

Enlarge to
106%
110%
for templates

The simple sardine outline drawings

59

• Creating a pattern

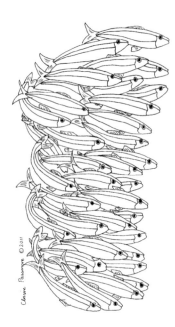

The shoal drawn using repeated fish shapes of different sizes

For the pattern I scanned the sketches and adjusted the size of the fish using PosteRazor (a photocopier would have been equally good). I experimented with many sizes, but eventually settled on enlarging the originals by 106% and 110% respectively. I then made lots of copies of the fish, but I could have just traced them many times or even drawn lots more freehand. For me, PosteRazor is just quicker.

With a large number of fish now ready I cut them out and began to arrange them on a large sheet of paper in various positions, angling and overlapping them to achieve an effect similar to that which I had seen in the National Geographic film. After much experimenting I found it easiest to use a large sheet of paper pinned to an even larger sheet of polystyrene bought from a local hardware store (I use this as a mobile design wall and also for blocking my finished quilts).

I pinned each of the small paper fish onto the larger sheet and moved them about, standing back from time to time to check how the composition looked. It was easy to see whether any of the fish needed to be moved or repositioned and whether any further alterations needed to be made to the shape or size of the fish. As it turns out the only changes I made were to the tails of a few fish on the edge of the shoal, to make them appear as though they were turning.

Once I was completely happy with the overall design I glued down the fish and took the whole sheet of paper to a local copy shop and had several full sized copies made to use as a pattern guide and templates (Unfortunately this shop has now closed down, so I now rely on Posterazor software for this step).

Tip

When making the full size copies of a design I usually make them in two formats - a straightforward copy and a mirror image copy. I pin the straightforward copy onto the design wall to use as a guide for positioning pieces and I cut up the mirror image copy to use as appliqué patterns.

• Design Principle: Harmony

This is a very clear example of how the use of repeated shapes brings harmony to a design. Slight variations in the size, shape and orientation of the fish shapes gives enough interest to stop the design looking boring (this is the contrast), but at the same time there is enough 'sameness' to bring order which is pleasing to the eye.

In the same way the virtually monochromatic color scheme also brings 'sameness' to the design which contributes to the harmony and unity in this quilt.

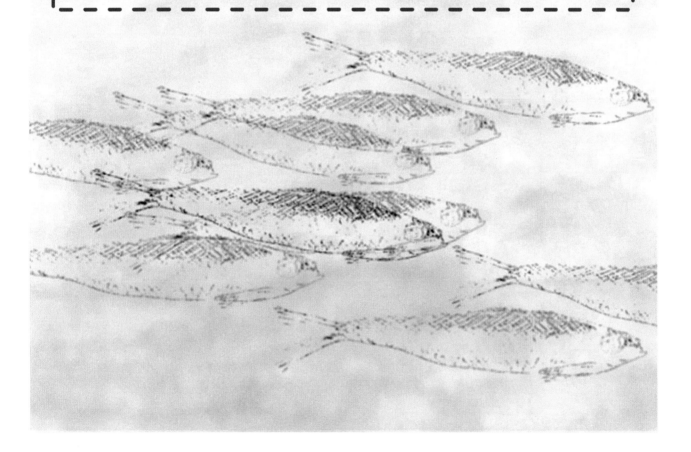

• Color Choices

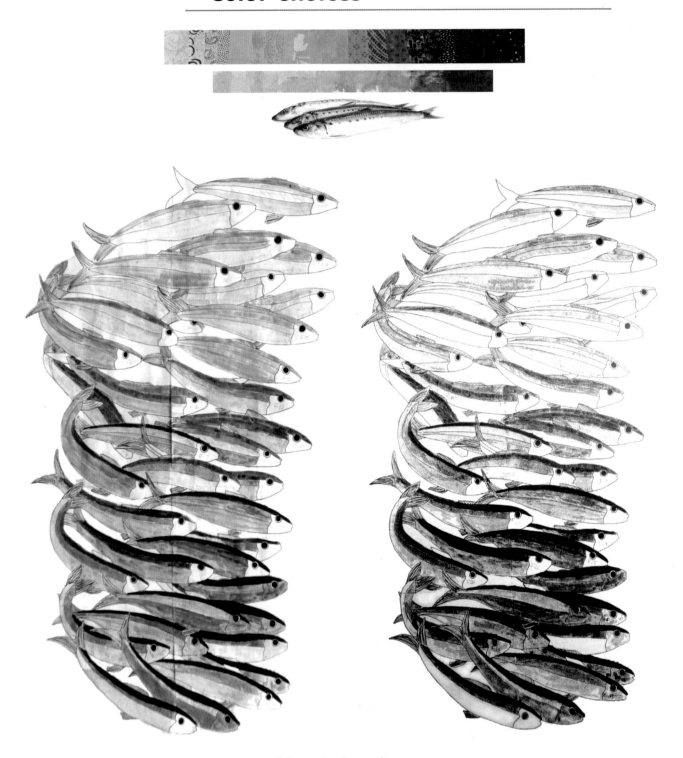

Color and value studies

• Color and Value

The color study from my sketchbook identified a very limited analogous color palette, from the gray/blue/green part of the spectrum with a good variety of values from very light through to very dark. Using this watercolor swatch I turned to my fabric stash and tried to find fabrics that matched as best as I could. From a large pile I eventually selected the fabrics on pages 65 and 71. Although many of the fabrics were not a perfect match I was able to find a large selection that I thought would be useful. I wanted to have as diverse a collection as possible to give lots of interest and variation between the large numbers of fish in the shoal. Auditioning them later on eliminated those that did not blend well, so at this point I included as many as I could.

Analogous colors: those that sit next to each other on the color wheel

From the Design Toolkit notes I had already decided that I wanted to try to capture the movement of the fish and the incredible luminosity of the water. Almost all of the pictures I have seen are taken from an angle below the fish, looking upwards towards the water surface. Apparently it is very difficult to capture these images, as the fish are moving so quickly and the close proximity of other large fast moving animals such as sharks, seals and dolphin mean it is quite a dangerous activity.

Being as much as 30 meters below the surface, light levels can be quite low, but as the camera is usually directed upwards, towards the light, the water appears to become lighter and brighter nearer the surface and the fish also appear to be lighter in color. I wanted to try to capture this quality in my quilt. To give me a better understanding of how to achieve this effect I used watercolor paints to paint one of the large copies of my pattern that I had made at the copy shop (See the picture, left).

Ask yourself

What sort of effect do I want? Do I want my fabrics to blend and merge, or do I want distinct differences to keep shapes discrete?

• Design Element: Value

Whilst looking closely at the real fish from the supermarket it was easy to see how the color and value changed on the different parts of their bodies. Replicating this with fabric demonstrates how using color in different values adds to a composition; the bands of light and dark on the different body parts of the fish contribute to that illusion of dimension. In addition, as the fish are positioned so closely, if adjacent fish were to be made from fabric with the same value they would simply merge into each other. The slight changes in value allow the observer to see each individual fish within the mass.

Added to this, the gradual change in value from the top to the bottom of the quilt, from the sunlit surface to darker depths, is an important design element. If the value remained the same the scene would once again lack the feeling of depth you get when looking upward or downward into water.

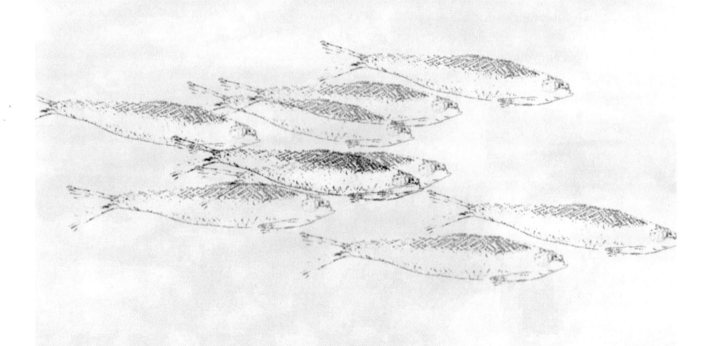

• Fabric Choices

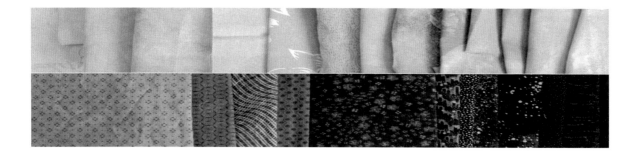

Whilst making the final choice of fabrics I decided I wanted to include a variety of hand dyed fabrics and commercial prints in order to provide a good mix of visual texture to the overall design. Since the bands of color on the real fish blended seamlessly into one another I thought it would be a good idea to over dye some of the commercial fabric prints with the same dyes I used for the hand dyed fabrics. This would mean they shared some of the color from the hand dyed fabrics and so could bridge the gap between the hand dyed and commercial prints, helping bring everything together. As it turned out this worked well and is something I will remember for future quilts when a blending of color and values is desirable.

• Dying the Fabrics

I started by mixing Procion MX type dyes (see page 170 for more information on these dyes) and dyed a selection of small pieces of plain, off-white 100% cotton fabric in a variety of very pale grays, blues and some sludgy gray-greens. I used 'Method 2' to dye the plain fabric as I wanted well blended colors. For exact details on the methods I use for dying fabric see page 149.

Once the first batch of fabrics was done I re-used the dye liquids, adding more water to lighten them even further, and over dyed some of the commercially printed fabrics. By brushing and dabbing the dye onto small pieces of soda ash soaked fabric I was able to control the process and create a good selection of shaded fabrics. The picture on the right shows a sample of the results. By using the same dyes to

Over dyed fabrics

dye the plain fabric as well as the commercial prints I was able to achieve lots of different values which blended perfectly. I just had to make sure I worked quickly and did not leave the fabrics soaking in the dye for more than 1 hour at a time since the soda ash was gradually degrading the dye bath all the time.

For the background fabric I used a slightly different technique. Looking at the images of the ocean I could see that the color quickly changed from a vibrant but pale watery turquoise at the surface to a deep, dark blue-black as the water became deeper. I also noticed tiny bubbles rising to the surface as the shoal swirled about. To try to replicate this effect for the wholecloth background fabric I decided to apply small dots of melted soy wax to a piece of 100% prepared for dyeing cotton fabric. To apply the wax I used a tjanting tool and carefully dotted the molten wax onto the fabric and then used the flat method to apply thickened dye. This wax formed a resist, stopping the dye from penetrating into the fabric, so leaving undyed white spots wherever the wax was placed.

Using 'Method 3' (page 164) with thickened dye, I mixed a number of different blue colors, from a vibrant turquoise to a deep, dark blue and spread the dampened fabric onto a large plastic sheet. Starting at the top of the fabric I brushed on a very pale thickened turquoise dye using a large, flat 1" decorator's paintbrush. Moving downwards I applied the remaining thickened blue dyes onto the fabric using deeper and darker shades and values of blue as I moved down the length of fabric. To stop there being definite stripes I needed to blend the dyes together just a little, so I brushed on a small amount of urea solution to help the different blue dyes mix and merge together. Once the dyeing process was finished and the fabric washed and dried, the soy wax was gone leaving tiny white spots on the graded blue fabric. The effect was good enough to be the foundation of the quilt, but it did not have the vibrant, luminous quality that I was looking for, so I knew I would need to experiment with other fabrics and techniques to try to find a solution to the problem. At this point, however, I was keen to make a start with the fish, so I left the blue background and began trying out ideas for the sardines.

Note: As an alternative to using the wax and dye, I could have chosen a suitable commercial print fabric for the background and added further detail with fabric paints – I just like messing about with dye, so that is the route I took.

Procion MX dyes

Turquoise
Midnight blue
Wedgewood blue
Camel
Gunmetal
Better black
Fuchsia
Lemon Yellow

Tjanting tools for applying melted wax

• **Testing Ideas**

Construction Techniques

With the fabric choices made and the pattern drawn and enlarged to the final size, I started to think about the construction methods I might use. I had recently purchased several books by the amazing quilt artist, Ruth B McDowell and had in mind trying the technique she describes for piecing complicated quilt tops. Using the excellent explanations in her book *Piecing Workshop (C&T 2007)* I decided to try and construct a sardine.

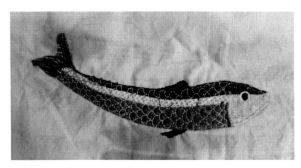

Pieced sardine shape appliquéd onto a blue background

I was very pleased with the results, but quickly realized I was biting off more than I could chew by attempting to create this quilt using this technique with my current skill levels. There were such a lot of overlapping small pieces in my design that I knew I would fail. I pondered redrafting the design to make it simpler and more manageable, but in the end I chose to keep the pattern as it was and try some other construction techniques. I am determined, however, to master Ruth B McDowell's technique!

I next tried fusing fabrics to the blue background. Using the mirror image copy of the pattern I traced a single fish onto a sheet of paper backed fusible web and cut it out, leaving a small margin around the outer edge of the fish, as you can see in the photograph below.

Using fusible web

Tip

Don't forget, when you use fusible web for appliqué you need to reverse the image before you trace it onto the web paper.

I cut the sections of the fish apart, cutting on the pencil lines, and fused each piece to the back of a selection of fabrics. The problem I found with this was that when I put the puzzle pieces back together there were often tiny gaps between the pieces, where my cutting had not been 100% accurate, allowing the background ocean fabric to show through. Whilst it was not terrible, I was not satisfied with the result. To solve this problem I decided to make sure I left a little excess fabric on the edges of some of the sections, so that they could slip under the adjoining pieces. Making sure I remembered where to leave this extra margin on each piece meant I would have to mark the pattern very carefully, but this was the only way I could see to ensure everything would be neat.

In the picture below you can see that wherever two or more fabrics touched I drew a red arrow to indicate that I would need to add a small allowance to the piece to allow it to slip beneath its neighbor. For the same reason I added a small extra area on the tail and fin sections, also highlighted in red, allowing this to slip beneath the body of the fish. I did this for every fish on the pattern so that when I was ready to begin construction I would know exactly how to cut every piece of fabric.

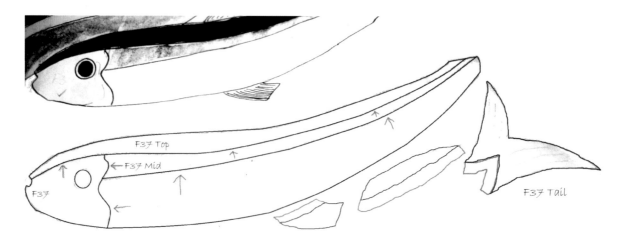

Adding cutting instructions to the pattern pieces. The red arrows indicate where I needed to add a small margin of fabric to the appliqué pieces.

Achieving depth of color and luminosity

Now I had decided how I was going to create the fish I returned again to exploring how to achieve the watery luminous effect I was aiming for. I experimented with layering sheer fabrics over the hand dyed background fabric. I tried adding layers of chiffon, tulle, voile and organza and after much playing about I found the shimmer and depth of color provided by overlapping layers of organza gave the effect I was looking for. I chose organza in 5 different values of blue and a bright white and cut them into uneven strips a few inches tall and slightly wider than the width of the background fabric. By slightly overlapping the strips of organza and placing the lightest values at the top, working my way downwards with increasingly darker values, I was able to grade the 'blueness' so that it appeared darker at the bottom of the fabric than at the top.

To see if I could improve upon this any further I then experimented with adding layers of net between some of the layers of organza. This added even more intensity to the color and enhanced the watery effect. By adding a little silver and white fabric paint to the quilted surface beneath the net I found a way to give an impression of the bubbles rising to the surface.

Layers of organza and net with added paint effects

Quite by chance I noticed that the edge of the small experimental piece that did not have any of the backing fabric beneath the organza and net also looked very attractive. I took advantage of this discovery later on when I came to finishing the edges of the quilt. (See page 79)

One problem I encountered with this layered effect was that there were many raw edges of organza which quickly began to fray, leaving strands of fine organza all over the place. To solve this problem I decided to neatly finish off the top layer of this experimental piece by placing a large single piece of net over the whole surface. By quilting this multi-layered fabric sandwich with a pattern of wavy horizontal lines I was able to keep all the loose pieces of organza together and trap the annoying fraying edges, giving a stable top layer.

Before starting work on the quilt, however, I had one further idea to explore; I decided to take advantage of the many layers of transparent fabrics by trapping a few sparkly sequins and Angelina fibers between the layers before I covered everything with the final top layer of net. I then quilted over the surface and captured the sequins in small pockets between the lines of stitching. The sequins did move about quite a bit during the process, and quite a few even fell out along the way, but I liked the overall effect of a few random highlights catching the light occasionally.

In the picture below you can also see that I tried a few different free motion quilting patterns: scallops, figures of 8 and loops, to see how they might look when I came to quilting the bodies of the fish.

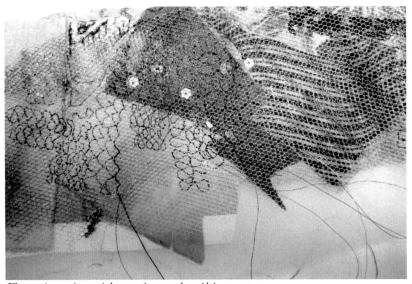

Experimenting with sequins and quilting patterns

• From Design to Quilt Construction

With the initial experiments now complete I began by starting work on the quilt top by carefully numbering each fish and all of its parts. With so many small pieces I did not want to risk ending up with a jumbled jigsaw puzzle of tails and fins. I must say, I was very glad I did as there were over 200 pieces!

Using the mirror image copy of the pattern I traced the fish, one at a time, onto the paper backed fusible web. I made sure to carefully think about how each fish was going to join or overlap each of its neighbors and marked this information onto the paper side of the fusible web. Sometimes there were up to 4 or 5 other fish adjacent to the one I was working on, but by being methodical and concentrating on only one fish at a time, I was able to trace and label each fish correctly.

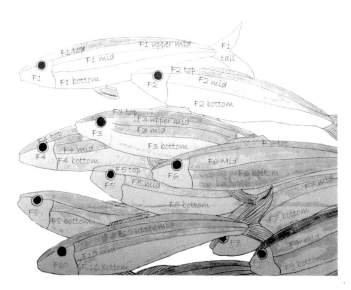

Labelling the quilt pattern

I next looked at the collection of fabrics I had sorted and chose dark, medium and light fabrics for each fish, being careful not to have two identical fabrics next to each other. I tried to mix the commercial prints with the over dyed and hand dyed fabrics so as to achieve a really good blend. I also made sure to select the very lightest fabrics for the fish grouped at the top of the quilt, as I wanted to make the shoal appear increasingly dark nearer to the bottom of the quilt.

> **Tip**
>
> Sort the final selection of fabrics according to value then cut a small sample of each and glue or stitch them into a strip. Use it to help guide you with your fabric selections for the fish.

Sorting the fabrics

With the fabric selections made, I next cut out the fusible web for one whole fish and cut it into its different sections. I fused each piece to its corresponding fabric and then cut it out using a very sharp pair of small scissors. I tried to be as disciplined as I could about working on one fish at a time so as to keep things organized. Sometimes, however, this just didn't work out and I needed to cut pieces from neighboring fish, so I was glad of the numbers and markings I had put onto each piece.

As each fish was completed I methodically pinned it onto the original copy of the pattern on the mobile design wall and began to build the shoal. In this way I was able to make sure I had the correct pieces next to each other, with the various parts overlapping correctly. I was also able to audition different fabrics to see which would be the best for any given position.

The shoal starting to take shape on my design wall

Once the whole shoal was cut and positioned I then pinned my blue background fabric onto a second design wall and began the process of transferring the fish onto the fabric. I removed one fish at a time, peeled off the backing paper, and with a very light touch of the iron, fused it to the blue background fabric. It was important to think about the order in which I should fuse the pieces, making sure to fuse the fabric that would lay behind other pieces first. It was a jigsaw puzzle in 3 dimensions, and sometimes I had to leave certain areas of fabric unfused, as I was going to need to slip another piece of fabric behind later. When this was the case I tried to keep a little of the backing paper still attached to the fabric in order to stop it from fusing to the background.

The shoal taking shape   *Grayscale photograph confirming the value mix*

When all the fish were temporarily fused in place I took the photograph above, then used my computer to turn it into grayscale to check that the values were graded as I had planned. Just to be sure I was happy with the arrangement and fabric choices I left it on the design wall for a few days and only when I was completely certain did I firmly press down all the pieces to ensure nothing moved.

• **Adding Dimension:** Machine Trapunto

To give the shoal more depth and to try to emphasize the relative position of each fish in relation to its neighbors, I decided to put an additional layer of batting beneath each fish. Using the simple technique of machine trapunto I was able to do this quickly and easily.

73

I began by placing a layer of thin 100% cotton batting onto the back of the quilt top, making sure there was batting behind all of the fish. I chose cotton batting as I find it clings nicely to the top fabric, reducing the chance of anything slipping or creeping as I outline stitched around the fish. However this technique will work with all types of batting, so use whichever you prefer or have available. **Note:** there is no backing fabric at this stage, just the quilt top and the batting layer.

I next placed a topstitch size 14/90 needle into the sewing machine and threaded it with water soluble thread in the needle and the bobbin. This is my usual needle choice for quilter's weight cotton, but obviously the fabric being used will influence your choices. If I have fine or silky fabrics I often move down to a size 12/80 or even a 10/70 needle.

I like to use water soluble thread for outlining the areas which will be raised by the extra batting beneath, as by the time the quilt has been completely quilted there can be quite a buildup of thread in these areas. If the extra stitching is part of the design then all well and good, but if not it can just look messy or bulky. By using soluble thread you can work quickly and not worry too much about being extremely accurate as you stitch around the shapes.

Using a free motion darning foot and with the feed dogs dropped, I outlined each fish with the soluble thread, sewing the blue background fabric as close as possible to the bodies of the fish. The purpose of these stitches was to temporarily hold the batting in place so that the excess could be cut away later. The overall effect gives each fish more definition and relief when compared to the background fabric.

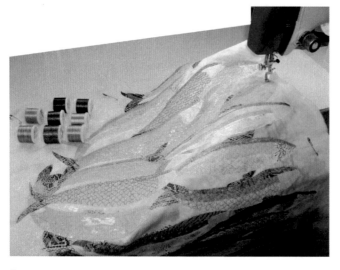

To enhance the effect further I chose to quilt a scalloped pattern onto the bodies of each fish to represent scales. I chose to do this now, rather than wait until I finally quilted the finished quilt top so that the visual texture on the fish and the water would be at different depths on the overall quilt.

Fish shapes outlined with water soluble thread then quilted with rayon and metallic threads

To make sure I liked the fish scale pattern I had chosen, I stitched it onto the original experimental fish I had created when deciding on my preferred construction technique (page 67). I selected some rayon and metallic threads and using ideas identified with the Design Toolkit I tried out a very simple row of scallop shapes that stacked on top of each other. The design was simple to stitch and looked very effective, giving good texture and rhythm. For the tails and fins I stitched simple straight lines. For the purpose of illustration it is easiest to see this pattern from the back of the quilt, below.

Stacking scallop pattern.

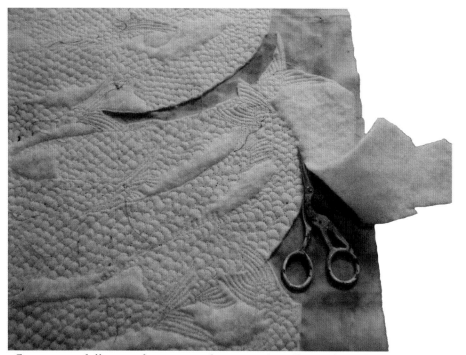

Cut very carefully to make sure you do not accidentally cut through the top layer of the quilt

Once all the fish were stitched and quilted the last thing to do for this step was to trim away the excess batting from around the outer edges of the fish. I took a lot of care with this, and using a pair of very sharp round nosed scissors I carefully cut away small sections of batting, pushing the scissors right up to the stitching line. I have tried many different pairs of scissors for this part of the process, including an expensive pair of duck billed scissors, but this is the method that works best for me.

Tip

Try out this technique with scrap fabric and batting before you attempt it on a quilt. It is easy to accidentally snip the quilt fabric as you trim away the batting.

• Adding Luminosity

Early in the development of this quilt I had experimented with layering organza and net, so I already knew which materials I would use for this effect. It also meant that this would be the last opportunity I had to add any further embellishment to the blue background fabric. So, before I started to layer on the transparent fabrics I used silver and white fabric paint to stamp small circles onto the blue background, to add to the appearance of small bubbles rising toward the surface. I used a small thin straw to dip into the paint and dotted it in small clusters. It was not a bold pattern, but it added subtle interest and visual texture to the water sections of the fabric.

Once the paints were dry I layered on the organza strips as I had done earlier. I also added small strands of Angelina fibers and sprinkled a few pale iridescent sequins randomly beneath the layers.

The effect of the different layers, fibers and sequins catching the light, was just the effect I was looking for and I continued playing about with the different elements until I found the most pleasing arrangement.

The only difficult issue I encountered with this construction method was with keeping the different pieces of light floaty fabric in place; they continuously shifted about and were difficult to control. The solution was to use temporary spray glue. I try not to rely on this product too much as I am not keen on the fumes, but under certain circumstances it has its uses, and this was certainly one.

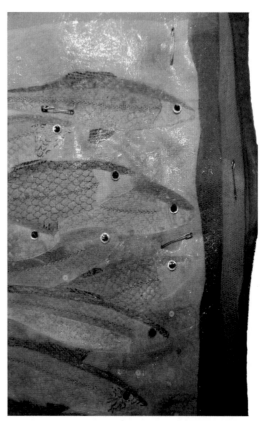

Layers of organza, Angelina fibers, sequins and net

In a well-ventilated room I gave the whole quilt top the very lightest mist of glue that I could manage and began to lay down the various layers, moving them about as necessary.

Using what I had learned in the experimental stages of this design I 'sealed' the many layers in place, laying an extra-large piece of very light blue net over the whole surface and pinned it all in place ready to quilt.

Tip

To make net and organza more manageable, iron it before use on a cool setting before you start work.

• Getting ready for quilting

Now the quilt top was ready I needed to prepare it for quilting. Since the edges of the quilt top were made from layers of transparent fabric the batting showed through and did not look attractive. To deal with this I decided to make a few changes to the way I prepared the quilt 'sandwich'. Firstly, I trimmed the batting and the backing fabric to the same size as the blue background fabric of the quilt top, rather than having it slightly larger as I normally would. Secondly I added an additional backing layer of blue net, cut to the same size as the net that covered the front layer. I wanted the net layers to form a capsule around the quilt, trapping everything inside, front and back. By having the net larger than the quilt left an unorthodox large flappy border which I decided to leave open and un-quilted. I was uncertain as to how I was going to bind this quilt and wanted to give myself options once the quilting was done.

The batting I chose was a medium-loft polyester, since I wanted the quilting stitches to sink into the batting and give more dimension than I would expect from a low-loft cotton or bamboo.

With all these layers in place I pinned the quilt all over with safety pins and got ready to quilt.

• Quilting Decisions

Happily, choosing a quilting design to finish this quilt was not a difficult task. The Design Toolkit had helped me to decide that I wanted a flowing, horizontal pattern to give the impression of moving water. I chose a simple undulating line design that was quick and simple to quilt.

Quilting lines

Undulating quilting lines

On scrap paper I sketched out rippling lines to confirm how dense and wavy I wanted them to look and also to let my hand practice the movement of the pattern.

For the thread I chose a variegated rayon in watery blue/green/yellow colors (Madeira Polyneon thread #1602) to add more depth to the color and a little more variation to the quilt top.

I started by outline stitching each fish one final time as I needed to trim away the layers of organza and net that covered them. I was glad I had used the water soluble thread to outline the fish earlier as I already had 2 lines of thread around each fish, which was quite noticeable. Fortunately I knew that once all the stitching was finished I could spritz the quilt with water and the line of soluble stitches would disappear.

Once the fish had been outlined with variegated rayon thread I started at the center-right of the shoal and quilted the gently undulating lines from right to left, stopping whenever I came to a fish and returning in the opposite direction a short distance away from the line of stitching I had just completed. I did not go beyond the edge of the blue quilt top fabric into the organza and net edging as I still had not made up my mind as to what to do with this section.

As I quilted I needed to take a little more care than usual as I moved the quilt under the needle so as to ensure all the layers were flat and that nothing had moved too much. I also needed to reposition some of the sequins a little with the tip of a pin, spreading them out under the net since they were quite mobile!

Once all the quilting was done I stood back and looked at the result. With all the layers of organza and net over the surface there was one unexpected consequence; I had not expected the transparent fabrics to subdue the fish quite as much as they did. Fortunately the solution was to simply trim away the organza and net covering the fish with sharp round nosed scissors, using a similar technique to the one I used to trim away the excess batting at the trapunto stage, revealing the vibrant fish once more.

Note: This time I trimmed away the fabric that covered the fish, not the fabric around the outside of the fish as with the trapunto.

• Finishing Details

I was very pleased with the way the quilt had finally come together, and one of the last things to do was to work on the eyes. At the start of the project I had created a pieced experimental fish and had stitched a small black circle surrounded by a white halo with rayon thread. It gave the impression of an eye, but was rather lifeless. Instead of settling for this I decided to leave the eyes until I had a chance to try and find something more suitable. As it turned out my patience was rewarded! Whilst browsing in one of my favorite haberdashery shops I came across a plastic tub filled with small discs of mother-of -pearl with a single tiny hole close to the edge. They could not have been more perfect. They were just the right size and the hole was perfectly placed for stitching them onto the fish. The only thing they lacked was a small black circle which I was able to paint onto the center of each disc. I bought a tiny tin of black gloss enamel model paint and spent a few hours carefully painting a circle onto each one. Once they were completely dry I was able to stitch them in place and the transformation of the quilt was incredible. The fish suddenly came to life. I could not have been happier!

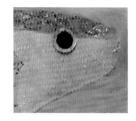

Painted Mother-of-pearl discs made great fish eyes

For the binding, I was also pleased that I waited. The effect of the flappy layers of net and organza gave a very soft edge to the quilt. After leaving the quilt on the design wall for a few days I finally decided to leave it as it was, without adding any further embellishment. With a pair of scissors I carefully sculpted the sides, trimming away fraying or jagged edges until I had pleasing gentle curves. It was the first time I had finished a quilt in this way and I was both surprised and pleased with the effect.

However, the real bonus came when I hung the quilt up to photograph. It was a bright sunny day and I had suspended the quilt from a hanging rail whilst it awaited its turn. With the sun behind, the whole quilt lit up and it really did seem luminous. Mission accomplished!

suggestions to try

- ✧ Explore using layers of transparent fabrics to see the different effects you can achieve
- ✧ Experiment with using different types of batting or layers of batting to add depth and dimension
- ✧ Try adding fabric paint and other embellishments to experimental pieces
- ✧ Let the piece guide you – if you aren't sure how to proceed, put the quilt on the wall and think about it for a while. Try to be patient
- ✧ Find inspiration and ideas by looking at how other people have achieved a certain 'look'

- ✧ Enjoy the process

'eGoli - City of Gold' **by Claire Passmore,** *18.5" x 40"*

Techniques

Cut work

Machine needle lace

Fabric dyeing

Fabric painting

Machine quilting

Design Focus

Balancing elements, line and texture

- Straight Stitch around letters, then cut out one piece at a time

- Zig-zag around 'hole'
  - stitch length between

  0 ↕ 1

  wwww 2/3

- Black thread on top
  Bobbinfil (black) under.

QUILTING   GOLD ribbon
                  cord
                  angelina fibres
                  binding
                  paints - fabric
                           oil sticks
                  tyvek
                  paper

contours

Rust - veins
paint

WEBS   Gold Thread
        Topstitch needle 90
Tips: keep speed high
Move fabric quickly
keep Up!
Don't let bobbin thread
loop up or catch

Business

CITY OF
GOLD

Fast Moving
Glorious Sunrises
Rough
Tough
High Rise
Busy - Hectic
Modern
Energy

WEBS
Stitch length 1
Tension   4 or 5
Gold thread in top & bobbin
Zig zag foot - (forward &)
                (reverse)

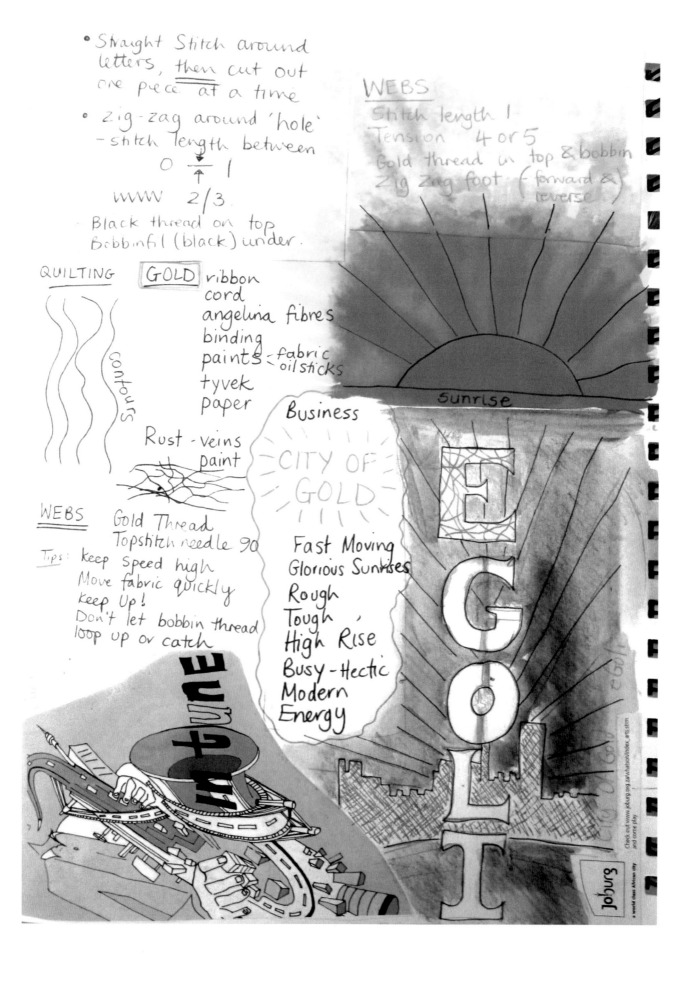

Sunrise

GOLT

Joburg

Check out www.joburg.org.za/whatson/index_arts.stm
and come play

a world class African city

• eGoli – City of Gold

Modern day Johannesburg is South Africa's biggest city by population. Amongst South Africans it has a reputation for being a vibrant, busy place with a focus on doing business. The people are friendly and laid back, making it an easy place to fit into. As in any city there is crime – and Johannesburg has more than its fair share, but is not true to say it is an inherently dangerous place; that rather depends on whom you talk to and where you go. It suffers, rather, from a bad image. My best friends live there, and love it!

Sunset over Johannesburg, illuminating the Sentech tower

Starting as a gold rush town in the 1860's it is known by many names; Jozi, Jo'burg, Joeys and my favorite, eGoli (pronounced ee–goal-ee, or ɛˈgəʊlɪ). eGoli comes from the Zulu word meaning 'Place of Gold' and this is the theme I decided to explore for this quilt.

• Sketchbook Inspiration

I knew from the start that I wanted this quilt to be based on gold. The roots of the city of Johannesburg are so linked to the unearthing of this precious metal hidden deep underground, that it seemed an obvious avenue to explore. I researched gold mining, rock formations and gold deposits and found some interesting images that gave me good ideas to work on. I also found a very nice image at the Johannesburg tourism office which I stuck onto my sketchbook page (left), where the artist had taken a cityscape and wound it around to form a saxophone shape. I really liked it, and it gave me the idea of incorporating the city skyline into the quilt.

On a blank sketchbook page I started by making a list of words of all the things that immediately came to mind when I thought of the word 'Johannesburg'. Staying with the theme of *gold* I decided to focus on the name eGoli and began to experiment with incorporating the name with ideas of gold seams, the rock beneath the city and the modern city itself.

When I revisited the sketchbook pages later that day I noticed that I had subconsciously drawn short lines around the word GOLD, much like the way an illustrator or cartoonist shows something in bright or shiny. It was not a deliberate design choice, but when I saw what I had done I realized that the lines may be a useful design element to incorporate into the finished design.

The scruffy sketch at the bottom right of the sketchbook page is the idea I chose to focus on for the quilt.

It demonstrates that you do not always need a beautiful image to get yourself started.

With just this small amount of work on the sketchbook pages I decided that it was time to use the Design Toolkit once again to see whether the framework could help me to pull my ideas together for the quilt.

Second sketchbook page for 'eGoli - City of Gold'

• **Color Choices**

Gold – obviously! To provide strong contrast and allow the gold to shine I knew I would need to use a dark background. This strongly influenced my color choices.

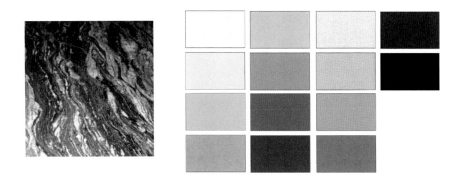

Inspiration and Color study made by matching paint chips

The inspiration for my color palette came from a beautiful piece of granite I saw on display at a local kitchen counter top supplier. I loved the intense darkness of the rock and the golden streaks that ran through it. It certainly had lots of drama!

With the store's permission, I took a photograph of the granite and used that to help create a color palette. I gathered together a selection of paint sample color chips (above) which I matched to the photograph. It was a very simple palette focusing on yellow and orange tints, shades and tones (see page 22 if you need a reminder of these color terms) and several dark grays, browns and black.

Analogous colors: those that sit next to each other on the color wheel

> ## <u>Ask yourself</u>
>
> Is 'gold' a color?
>
> The short answer is no, gold is not a true color. What we think of as shiny gold is actually yellow mixed with a very small amount of red to warm it up a little and then mixed with reflective materials to create the impression of real gold.

• Using the Design Toolkit

Design Toolkit© for Quilters - elements

Lines	Shapes	Space	Colors	Textures
	 Organic freeform 2D shapes Geometric 2D shapes	 Positive Space Negative Space	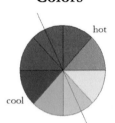 hot cool	 Texture
Thick, thin, straight, curved, zig zag, horizontal, vertical, diagonal, continuous, broken, dotted.............. Pay attention to why you drew the lines and what they might be showing	2 dimensional flat shapes are made from lines which have been joined up They are either geometric or organic	The area around, within or between shapes or parts of shapes Important for perspective. Can be positive or negative	Hues, Shades, Tints, Tones, Values Color and Value studies help with this element	Can be physical or visual, real or implied Makes use of threads, different fabrics and patterns or prints

Johannesburg city skyline – outline of the tall buildings in the CBD

Capital letter shapes for the word   EGOLI

Big and bold to reinforce idea of strength and importance

Sunrise – shiny gold / sunrise over the city – divides the background into sections. How to use these lines/ sections???

Streaky lines of gold – make with fabric, thread, paint or hand embroidery
Try creating strands of gold metallic thread to create thin floating golden lines

Shape of the city skyline – outline with thread and fill the space inside with gold fabric paint.
Space around city – sunrays?   Space below the city, gold

'eGoli' letters – how can I make them gold but different???   Organza over top / appliqué / cut out to leave negative shape / fill with thread sketching / dense quilting with gold thread / pierce with soldering iron tip to make small holes / paint /foil/ fill with hand stitching ??? Experiment.

Color –Gold and lots of it. To give maximum contrast also use lots of black Add other accents of earthy colors to give a feeling of being underground. Need something light in value to give more contrast

Hand dye fabric to achieve a rocky irregular appearance with streaks of gold
Smooth hard shiny texture of gold – fabric paint and flat surface for the city
Rough hard texture of rock underground – lots of dense quilting to give uneven knobbly surface for the rock

Design Toolkit© for Quilters - principles

(Toolkit for placing design elements)
www.clairepassmore.weebly.com

Harmony	Contrast and Dominance	Rhythm	Balance	Unity
				Overall arrangement of lines, shapes, colors and/or textures complement each other
Repeated lines, shapes, patterns, colors, motifs or textures	Variation of lines, shapes, colors, textures, orientation.	Predictable and organized order of lines, shapes, patterns textures colors or motifs	Elements arranged so that visual weight is balanced, symmetrical, radial, asymmetrical, mosaic, big balanced by many small, or small bright shape balanced by larger dull shape	Nothing appears out of place and there is consistency within the design
Gives calmness and is easy on the eye. Too much can be boring	Think of opposites, e.g. light and dark. Gives importance, impact & variation	Can be regular, progressive, alternating or flowing. Helps guide the eye.		Grouping and/or repeating elements contributes to unity as does continuing lines, shapes, colors, textures or techniques throughout the design

Gold, deep underground beneath the tall modern city of Johannesburg. City of sunrises

Try to limit to 3 elements only – skyline, letters and sunrise. Name of city to be most important so needs to be made more dominant   Big, bold golden color, central or at focal point
Use capital letters so all are roughly same size and more uniform shape than if I use lower case letters (Also more formal and 'strong')
Position them in a formal row or column – column would possibly give feeling of physical depth underground?

Repeated use of stitched line for sunrise – regularly spaced and focusing the eye inwards to a focal point.   **E**
What should go between them? Very understated quilting pattern so as not to distract from the rays or   **G**
other elements   **O**
Centre of the city at the focus point of rays or maybe center of the letter O?   **L**
      I

Background areas - repeated quilting pattern all over the rock sections of the quilt to give 'rough' texture

Contrast of color – black and gold
Contrast of texture – rough rock and smooth gold

Horizontal orientation of the cityscape could be balanced by something vertical. EGOLI letters vertically would solve this
Sunrays radiating from city suggest radial balance. How to bring horizontal vertical and radial together? Keep it symmetrical!

Limit the color palette so as not to introduce too much variety. Black, Gold (shiny or matt??) beiges or creams to give contrast in value

• Design Principles: Dominance and Balance

This quilt demonstrates how a dominant design element can be balanced with other elements to ensure the overall design is both unified and harmonious.

Dominance can be achieved by contrasting design elements in several ways; by contrasting the size, color, position and shape of the various design elements you use some elements become more prominent than others.

Balance concerns the way elements are distributed around a quilt. There are 4 general arrangements: Symmetrical; Asymmetrical; Circular; Mosaic (also known as all over patterns or crystallographic balance).

By using the word 'EGOLI' in large capital letters and placing it vertically down the center of the quilt it became the focal point; that is to say that as soon as you look at the quilt this is what immediately captures your attention, dominating the piece. But a quilt with just a single element is quite likely to be rather boring and after a glance the viewer would move on. The quilt needed more 'interest', so more elements needed to be added, and if you add more elements these need to be balanced to make the quilt visually appealing.

Here I used size (large capital letters) and position (straight down the center) to create the dominant element.

Balance has been achieved by placing a smaller horizontal element in the bottom third of the quilt. The eye is first drawn downwards, and then across the quilt. This is an example of asymmetrical balance. By adding quilting lines that radiate outwards from the intersection of those vertical and horizontal elements radial balance has been added to the quilt. Overall the quilt has a formality and feels balanced and unified.

• Developing the design

Although there was not much in the way of detail on the sketchbook pages, I was pleasantly surprised at how the prompts in the Design Toolkit helped me to extract lots of ideas for the quilt both quickly and easily.

I began developing this design by considering the 3 main elements the tool kit had helped me focus on: the word 'eGoli', the city skyline and the sunrise. To balance the horizontal layout of the city skyline I decided to layout the name 'eGoli' vertically. I liked the simplicity of the name of the city standing out, so I chose large capital letters. I also wanted to reinforce the idea that the gold was deep down in the rock beneath the city, and laying out the letters this way gave me a long thin design which made a tall, narrow, rectangular quilt.

Positioning the skyline within this long thin design needed some careful consideration. Placing it near the top of the rectangle (and therefore allowing me to show the deep nature of gold bearing rock below the city) looked very strange; it made the city appear as if it was flying! I really didn't like that effect, but placing it near the bottom (where our eye expects the ground to be), meant I lost the idea of being deep underground the city. I struggled to find a way to get this deepness across and eventually I thought about making the letters look as though they had been cut out of the rock. I knew I would need to try this idea out, as I had never cut into a quilt before, but the idea seemed promising and opened up a whole new avenue of ideas in terms of the construction technique.

Positioning the design elements

I decided that if this idea worked I would keep the city skyline towards the bottom of the quilt and then use the final element, the sunrise, to radiate out from the city.

• Pattern Templates

As this was such a simple design, essentially just a rectangle containing large letter shapes and a skyline, I chose not to make a large paper pattern of the whole quilt. Instead, I decided on the dimensions of the final quilt and created templates for the shapes I required.

The only templates I needed were for the letters of the word EGOLI and the city skyline. Using a word processor I identified several potential fonts and selected one that had lots of open space inside the letters. To calculate the font size required I experimented by printing samples of the letters in different sizes and spent some time with paper and scissors to find a pleasing size to fit the dimensions of the quilt. I ultimately selected the following: Font name '*Stencil*', size 500 in bold.

Once I had printed out the letters I cut them out and they became the paper templates I used to mark the quilt top. For the cityscape template I simply drew freehand using the image from my sketchbook as a reference.

Johannesburg skyline

• Testing Ideas

In the back of my mind I knew that for some time I had wanted to try using cutwork and machine needle lace in a quilt project. Once the idea of cutting into the quilt had emerged, the letters of the word 'eGoli' seemed the perfect place to experiment with these techniques. In my spirit of 'just go for it' I layered up some scraps of fabric and batting and started stitching and cutting. I was pleased to find that it is not at all difficult to make simple webs across a space with a sewing machine, and I was quickly able to achieve a look that made me think of spider webs or veins. I am sure any person experienced in this technique would look on in horror as I used no hoop or stabilizer, but for my purposes it worked well, so I was a happy quilter! If you try out this technique I suggest you experiment to see whether you need the extra stability of a hoop or soluble stabilizer and keep notes of the stitch width, length and tension settings you use.

Tip

Keep notes of machine settings from your experiments in your sketchbook, or pin a piece of paper with the notes onto your samples.

Initial experiments with cutwork and needle lace

The vein like threads immediately reminded me of the streaks of gold in the kitchen counter top picture I had stuck in my sketchbook, and I decided I was definitely going to use this interpretation of the technique for the quilt. Details of how I created the needlelace are on page 94.

The benefit of trying out new techniques and experimenting also led to another unexpected result; I had not given any thought to what lay behind the hole created by the cutwork, as I was completely focused on filling the empty space with thread! What I discovered, rather obviously in retrospect, was the importance of what lay behind the open space, enabling the needle lace threads to show up. To deal with this issue I decided to make a second quilt to suspend behind the original to provide a contrasting backdrop.

As well as fine tuning techniques and ideas, experimenting before you start also helps identify possible pitfalls and things you may have missed in the design process.

How could I have not realized I would need a second quilt to suspend behind the open cutwork of the first????

• Fabric Choices

With most of the decisions on how to progress with the quilt now made I felt it was time to choose the fabrics I would use.

Whilst using the Design Toolkit I had identified that I wanted to incorporate gold in lots of different ways on the quilt, in the form of metallic paints, threads and fabrics. I already had one piece of fabric in mind which I thought may be suitable, a very dark, almost black fabric with a vibrant gold print. It seemed perfect, and realizing I would now need a second quilt as a backing to the first, I set this aside for that purpose.

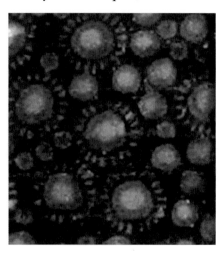

A black and gold print I reserved for the backing quilt

The simple color study provided me with a color palette and the piece of dark, streaky granite had inspired me to try dyeing a piece of fabric that would have a similar streaky effect to represent the rock. To achieve the streaked look I used 'Method 1' to apply the dye to a twisted length of fabric. See pages 149 – 165 for the exact details of the dyeing methods I often use.

Using an off-white 100% cotton prepared for dyeing fabric, I pre-soaked it in soda ash solution so that the dye would begin to fix straight away and the colors would not merge too much. I loosely pleated the fabric along its length and laid it out on a large plastic sheet, trying to keep the pleats as irregular as possible. I then gave it 3 loose twists, as if I were wringing it out, and placed a stone on each end to stop it from unraveling. Trying not to disturb the pleats too much I used small pipettes to squirt different dyes onto the fabric. By squirting the dyes down the length of the twisted fabric I was able to create the long streaked patterns I was aiming for and to ensure I had enough contrast in value I used more light colors of dye than dark.

I then covered the pleated and twisted length of fabric with another sheet of plastic to stop it drying out and left it in the sun until the next day. When I eventually unrolled it I was very happy with the effect so I rinsed, washed and dried the fabric ready for use.

Hand dyed streaky rock fabric for the quilt

• From Design to Quilt Construction

Once the rock fabric was finally ready I layered up the quilt using a medium loft polyester batting and 100% cotton poplin backing. To keep the layers together for the quilting process my preference is to use lots of safety pins, but spray glue, tiny plastic tacks or basting stitches also work well. I strongly believe it is important to find the methods that suit you and not worry about the so called 'right' way to do things. For small project spray glue is often practical, so use what works for you and your project.

To prepare for free motion quilting I thread my sewing machine with the same thread in the needle and bobbin and use an open toed darning foot so that I can see exactly where I am stitching. When using metallic or rayon threads I prefer to use topstitch needle, which I find reduces thread breakage and shredding. I also always put the thread onto a thread stand behind the machine to give the thread room to unwind. Using a variegated brown and caramel thread I began by free motion quilting around some of the shapes created by the dye, outlining the boundary lines between the dark and light areas. If you look closely at the picture above you can see the stitched lines.

Tip

With delicate threads try a topstitch needle, size 80/12 or 90/14.

Put the thread onto a stand behind the machine to reduce tangles and thread breakage.

• Cutwork and Needlelace

Outlining the letters with short stitches

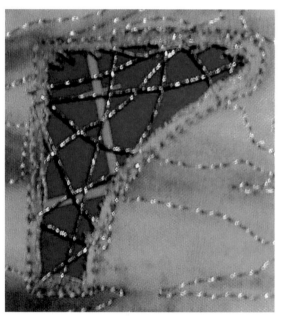

The hole cut in the fabric, showing the outline stitching and the needlelace webs

With the quilt layers secured I positioned the paper letter templates I had prepared earlier onto the quilt top. I found the center by folding the fabric in half lengthwise and marked it with a line of chalk. I laid the templates along the line, spacing them evenly, and drew around them with a chalk pencil before removing them. With an open-toed foot on the machine and a light brown thread in the bobbin and needle I stitched along the outlines using a shorter than usual stitch length which gave a firm, stable foundation edge to the letters.

Starting with the letter E, I carefully cut out the fabric from inside the smallest section of the letter. I cut as closely as I could to my stitched line, making sure to cut carefully into the corners and around the curves. I used a very small pair of sharp, pointed scissors to ensure I was accurate and had no mishaps.

I next changed the foot on my machine to a closed darning foot, and dropped the feed dogs. If your machine does not have this function, then do not worry. One of my machines has a small plastic plate that is used to cover over the feed dogs, but I find it too thick and lumpy under the fabric so instead, I use a piece of thin card. I cut a small hole in the center for the needle to pass through and stick it onto the sewing machine bed with masking tape. As always, use whichever method you find works best for you.

Making sure I had the topstitch needle in the machine I threaded up with a metallic gold thread in the needle and bobbin. As I had practiced this technique during my experimental phase I had already found the best tension, stitch length and stitching speed to use to ensure the best results. For my machine, with this thread, I used the following:

Stitch Length 1

Tension 4 or 5 (it varied?!?)

Closed darning foot

Using the stitched line around the hole in the fabric as a guide, I put the needle down into the quilt fabric and pulled up the bobbin thread. I then held both the needle and bobbin threads securely to the side and began to stitch across the void, moving the quilt with my hands as if I were free motion quilting. Through my earlier trials I discovered that I needed to keep the speed of stitching quite fast as when I tried to sew more slowly the threads tangled and the machine jammed. By sewing quickly, however, the loops of thread formed quite quickly too, so I needed to keep the quilt moving to keep up. I am sure you will discover your own method, but for my machine, keeping the speed quite fast was important to keep up with the rate at which the machine was producing the line of thread. If I let the thread loop up or catch up with me then that is when the problems began. It sounds as if it was difficult, but it really wasn't.

Once I had found my rhythm I was able to sew across the void very easily, landing in a new position on the stitched line around the edge of the letter each time. The fun part was that it did not matter which direction I moved the quilt, going back and forth from one side of the void to the other to form the web of golden threads.

Gradually working on one small section at a time, I cut out and stitched the needlelace into the empty letter spaces. By only cutting one section at a time the quilt was still quite stable and easy to handle. The only difficulty I encountered was with the letter 'O' where the central part of the letter was very thin, so I needed to take extra care and keep the quilt taught whilst stitching here.

Once all the needlelace webs were complete I replaced the darning foot with the zigzag foot, raised the feed dogs and rethreaded the machine with a thin black bobbin-fill thread in the needle and bobbin.

Tip

Make a note on your sketchbook pages of the settings you have used during your experimental stage. You will be glad you did when you start to make your quilt!

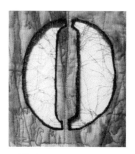

Take care around the thin section of the letter 'O'

Using a zigzag stitch I satin stitched around the letter outline once again, sealing up the raw edge and covering the line of foundation stitches I put in place earlier. When I needed to turn a corner I left my needle down on the outside edge of the zigzag, pivoted and carefully began to sew again. As these were all inside corners it was not at all difficult. For the curves I simply steered the quilt around, slowing down my sewing speed a little to help me keep control.

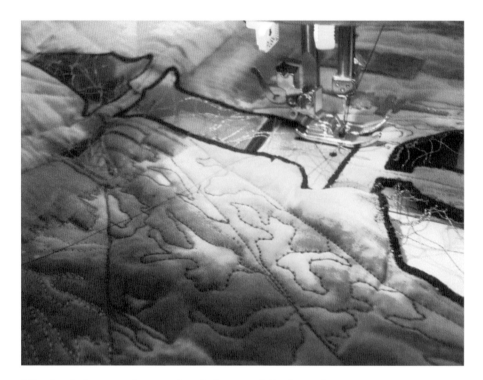

The final edging – zigzag satin stitch around the letter shapes

For the satin stitch edging I used the following settings:

Stitch length between 0 and 1

Stitch width between 2 and 3

Zigzag foot

• Using painted fusible web

My intention had been to use only stitch to add the skyline to the quilt surface and then use fabric paints to infill the stitched line. During the construction process I painted over this area 4 times with gold fabric paints and was always unhappy with the results. Initially it was too dull, as I had chosen dark gold fabric paint. I went over it with a bright gold, but that was so vibrant it took over the entire quilt, making the skyline such a strong focal point that the rest of the quilt faded away. I struggled with this for several days and finally decided to hang the quilt on my design wall and leave it alone. I needed time to think and work out what to do. I knew I needed to mute the gold in some way – the problem was how?

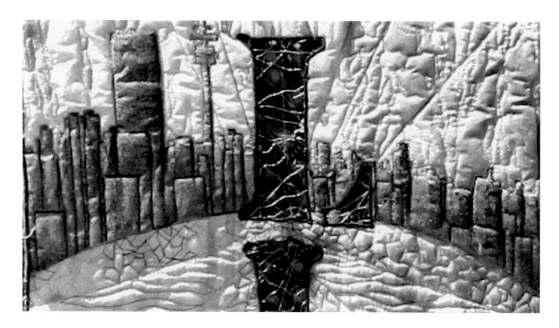

The city skyline painted gold and muted with painted fusible web

In the end I solved the problem very simply. I painted over a piece of paper backed fusible web (the type that we use for fusing appliqué) with black artists' acrylic paint and let it dry. It wrinkled up a little and was quite patchy in appearance, but it was still manageable. I then traced the outline of the skyline onto the paper side, cut it out and carefully fused it over the gold painted skyline. When I peeled away the backing paper, the skyline was instantly muted, enough to stop it taking over, but not too much to make it dull. Problem solved! I just need to remember to *NEVER* touch this section with a hot iron.

> **Tip**
>
> Try to think of all the materials you have to hand and using them in different ways to solve problems. Don't be afraid to experiment.

• Quilting Decisions

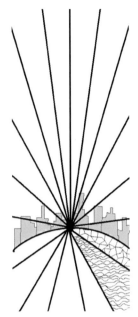

Trying out ideas for quilting patterns and lines

With the cutwork, needlelace and skyline completed I returned the quilt to my design wall once again and considered it for a week or so. I wanted to mull over what else it might need. The quilting that outlined the dark and light areas of the quilt did give a rock like texture – but it was an allover design and although interesting, was a little flat. I wanted something to give the quilt some more energy, to pull everything together and unify it.

As mentioned earlier, the word 'EGOLI' provided a very strong vertical element and the cityscape a less dominant horizontal element. To help me work out what would look best I made a very rough sketch and experimented with putting pieces of tracing paper over the top, experimenting with the position and orientation of different lines. The arrangement that I liked best was of straight lines radiating outwards from the center of the city skyline, so I marked out the lines with a soluble pen, put the walking foot onto my machine and quilted them with gold metallic thread and a straight stitch.

For the area below the skyline I decided to reinforce the idea of being below the ground by altering the visual texture of the quilt. Using the tracing paper method once again I experimented with different quilting patterns and chose two contrasting patterns to alternately fill the sections between the rays I stitched earlier.

Angular rock shaped quilting

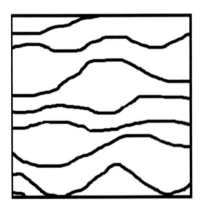

Curved strata quilting design

• Design Principle: Unity

The need to unify two quilts into a single piece of work was an unexpected challenge for this quilt. Bringing together all the elements in any design is essential. I think of it as tying everything together– whether that is just the collection of elements you have in a single quilt or, as in this case, two separate quilts.

This unity can be achieved in several ways. Here are a few:

grouping elements together – known as PROXIMITY

using similar elements from one section in another – known as SIMILARITY

extending a line, pattern or shape – known as CONTINUATION

repeating elements many times – known as REPETITION

The solution I chose to unify these two quilts was to select similar colored fabrics and threads and to extend and continue the quilting lines from the top quilt out onto the second rear quilt. At the base, below the skyline I repeated the quilt filler pattern too.

• The Backing Quilt

Now that the top quilt was more or less finished, I pulled out the black and gold fabric I had reserved earlier. It was a perfect contrast to the hand dyed fabric I used for the top quilt and showed through the needle lace well, having enough gold to contrast with the front quilt and make it pop. Just to be certain I pinned the fabrics onto my design wall, placed the quilt on top and took a photograph, which confirmed my choice.

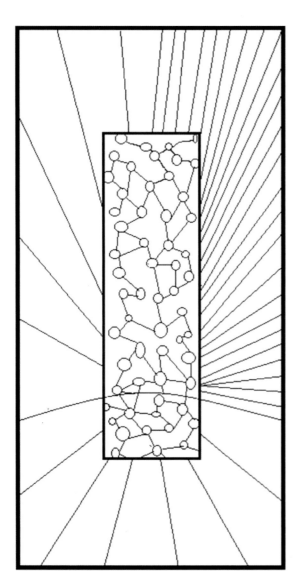

As I had not originally planned for this quilt I had nothing in my sketchbook to refer to. However, I had been mulling over what to do with it ever since I realized I was going to need a background quilt. I knew I did not want to make anything complicated that would detract from the top quilt so I placed the fabric and quilt on my design wall and stared at it for a while – waiting for inspiration! Fortunately, the solution was obvious. The flow of the rays that I had quilted onto the top quilt called out to be extended onto the background. This not only unified the two quilts but also added to the starburst effect emanating from the skyline, or pointing inwards like many arrows, depending on your point of view.

To decide the size of the quilt I folded the fabric and experimented with different dimensions and I finally settled on a rectangle measuring 18 ½" x 14" as it looked most balanced. Obviously this is not the ideal way to make a quilt if it is to be for a specific position, but getting the correct proportions is important if it is to look 'right'.

Quilting design for the back quilt

100

With the fabric cut just a little larger than I needed, I laid the eGoli quilt onto the fabric and placed my long ruler onto the ray lines I had already quilted, extending them onto the new quilt top. With light colored chalk I marked the lines so they would match up with those on the eGoli quilt. Because the rays diverged, by the time they arrived at the edge of the quilt they were rather too widely spaced so I decided to add extra ray lines radiating from the same central point. This added even more texture to the second quilt top and gave a very strong visual element, focusing the eye inwards and outwards from the central point on the skyline.

Once the top was marked I layered the quilt as usual and pinned it ready for quilting. For the straight ray lines I used a walking foot, a metallic gold thread in the needle with a topstitch 12/80 needle and a thin black thread in the bobbin.

For the central area that would be covered by the top quilt I chose to section it off and quilt it more densely, as I wanted it to be flatter than the exterior part which formed the border to the original quilt. In the diagram on page 100 you can see the central panel quilted with small circles joined by straight lines. I arrived at this pattern by using the print on the fabric itself. The fabric print had small gold circles all over, so I quilted around each circle then branched off to travel to the nearest neighboring circle in a continuous design. It is a quick and easy filler that works well in almost all areas of most quilts and has become one of my favorites. I used the same thread combination as for the rays, but dropped the feed dogs, changed to a darning foot and free motion quilted the circles connected by straight lines in one continuous line.

For the section below the skyline I repeated the quilting I had done on the top quilt using the rock and strata lines, helping to unify the two separate quilts.

• Finishing Details

Now both quilts were complete I needed to decide on the finishing techniques for the edges. One of the most important things I have learned as a quilter is to be patient and not make hasty decisions. Unpicking is not one of my favorite pass times! With both quilts in front of me my decision was 'to bind, or not?' I decided I did not want a strong line of color or fabric around the edge of the top eGoli quilt as that would make a hard visual boundary between the two quilts. For that reason I decided to finish it with a simple satin stitch edging to seal the edges neatly.

After trialing different methods on scraps of fabric I chose not to use any stabilizer around the edges of the quilt for this process. I considered using a soluble stabilizer to keep everything in check, but happily, the quilting that was already in place was sufficient enough to keep the layers of the quilt together and stop any unwanted movement. I also found that by slightly reducing the pressure on the foot the quilt moved through the machine smoothly.

During my trials I also discovered that it was best not to start stitching at a corner, but to begin stitching about 2 inches or so in from the corner and commence the circuit from there. To achieve a neat finish I stitched around the quilt 3 times in total, using a zigzag foot and a zigzag stitch, with black thread in the bobbin and in the needle. For the first tour around the quilt I used a narrow stitch width and longer length than on the subsequent rounds, just to make sure the edges were neatly sealed.

The corners were a little more challenging to get neat, so by starting a little way in I was able to control the stitching more easily. I tried several methods for turning the corners before I found something that reliably gave a neat finish. I tried sewing right up to the very edge of the quilt, left the needle down on the outside of the stitch and pivoted, as I had done earlier when finishing around the letter shapes. However, as this was an outside corner there was no fabric on the right hand side of the feed dogs and I initially found my machine did not want to smoothly take the fabric through and continue sewing. I next tried using a small piece of soluble stabilizer that extended beyond the quilt edges at the corner to allow me to grab the excess and gently pull the quilt to get it started again. This did work, but was quite fiddly. By far and away the quickest and simplest way I found was to take a stiletto (I use an old blunt dart) and *very* carefully place it onto the fabric, just to left of the needle, making sure it did not interfere with the path of the needle in any way. When I started to sew again just a little push on the stiletto was enough to get the fabric sewing smoothly and made a neat line of satin stitch. I can only emphasize that you need to be extremely careful if you do this as you risk breaking the needle or pushing the dart down into the feed dogs,

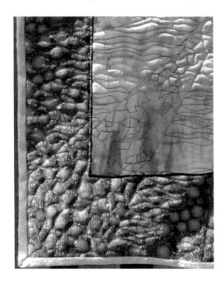

The two different binding finishes I chose for the quilts

so proceed with the greatest care. I recommend trialing various methods before you decide on your favorite, as each machine is different. It might well be that you are lucky enough that your machine does not have an issue with this!

For the edge finishing of the back quilt I did not want to replicate the satin stitch. This is a good technique for small quilts that would look too heavy with a conventional binding, or if you do not want a definite hard or contrasting edge, but for the larger backing quilt I wanted something more definite. I decided to use a conventional binding method, but instead of fabric I chose a piece of dull gold ribbon. It was 1.5" wide and fairly coarse in texture and gave a good firm edge to the quilt. It was the first time I had used ribbon to bind a quilt and it turned out to be a very simple and effective choice and finished off the piece perfectly.

suggestions to try

✧ Always try out ideas and techniques on the same fabric as your quilt before you commit to using them on your work

✧ Keep notes of the settings you use in your experiments

✧ Experiment with cutting holes into a small quilted square and try filling it in different ways

✧ Layer quilted fabrics for different effects

✧ Try different ways of finishing quilts other than traditional binding

✧ Try using different needles with speciality threads to see which you prefer

✧ Sample different thread combinations for different effects

✧ Explore the different feet you have for your machine and find out what you can achieve with each one. Don't be limited by what the manual says!

✧ Try painting fusible web and experiment with how it can be used

✧ Enjoy the process

'Bunny Chow' by Claire Passmore, 16 ½" x 25"

Techniques

Raw edge appliqué

Machine trapunto

Free motion quilting

Laminating transparent fabrics

Design Focus

Telling a story with color, shapes and text

• Bunny Chow

Bunny What???

Yes, you read it correctly! If you are a South African, or have been lucky enough to visit this beautiful country, then you will surely know exactly what Bunny Chow is. If not..... read on.

Bunny Chow or more colloquially known simply as 'Bunnies' are a spicy, delicious, rather messy type of street food that has a huge fan base throughout South Africa, but especially in the vibrant city of Durban. As long as you have a good strategy to tackle the way you eat it you will be rewarded with a delicious and hearty meal. In its simplest form it consists of a fiery Durban-style curry sauce ladled into a hollowed out loaf of bread; giving a portable meal to be eaten, well, anywhere! Depending on how hungry you feel you can order a quarter, half or whole bunny, the size being dictated by the size of the loaf of bread you want. The center of the loaf is removed, the curry ladled into the void and the extracted bread placed back on top of the now over brimming loaf. As your Bunny comes wrapped in yesterday's newspaper, be sure to support the base, especially if you are given the 'Funny Bunny' – the portion of the loaf that came from the center and therefore does not have the crust to support all that lovely curry sauce.

A quarter bunny. It may not be the most beautiful dish in the world, but it tastes delicious!

Photograph by Luke Comins, Wikimedia Commons, 2010

Originally a vegetarian dish, the Bunny has been transformed over time to contain anything from a traditional Durban-style curry using mutton, lamb, chicken or fish, a spicy dhal – or a cheaper culinary twist; beans and chips!

Each September a competition is held, known as the 'Bunny Chow Barometer' at a popular picnic spot in Durban to determine who makes the best Bunny in town. So now you know where to head next time you need a snack!

• Sketchbook Inspiration

As a quilter I am always looking for inspiration for future projects and this time it arrived on a plate!

Whilst visiting Durban on a short vacation I could not possibly have left without trying an authentic Bunny. I searched the internet for the *Best Bunny Guide* and was soon enjoying a superb 'quarter mutton'. This was all the inspiration I needed for my next quilt project. For the remainder of the afternoon I sat with my sketchbook and let my pencil and watercolors do the talking.

Since bunny chow is not terribly well known outside South Africa I decided to focus on letting others know what this tasty food is all about and made two pages in my sketchbook. The first was a cartoon style play on the name 'Bunny Chow' with a funny rabbit popping his head out of a loaf of bread. It was fun to draw, but it didn't give many further clues to the uninitiated as to what bunny chow is and so was actually pretty useless as a visual description.

My second page was much more explicit. I decided to try to write a simple recipe to tell the story and as I was still in a cartoon mood I chose the style of an illustrated recipe, the kind you might find in a child's recipe book. It is this page that I decided to use as the basis for the quilt.

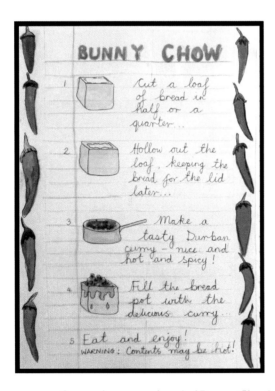 

So, you have never heard of Bunny Chow? What could it be?

• **Design Element: Color**

Color theory identifies numerous color schemes which are most easily seen using a color wheel, but for practical purposes here are the most straightforward combinations:

Monochromatic: A single hue with variations in value. For example: red pink, burgundy …….Easy on the eye, clean, elegant and calm but lacks contrast. *The quilt 'Sardine Run' makes use of this color scheme.*

Analogous: 2 or more adjacent colors on the color wheel. For example: red, orange, and yellow. Rich and harmonious but still lacks contrast. *This is mostly what I used for this quilt.*

Complimentary: 2 colors on exact opposite sides of the color wheel. For example: red and green. A lively combination that gives energy and maximum contrast and always looks harmonious. *I took advantage of this combination by adding small amounts of green to my color palette for this quilt.*

Triadic: As the name suggests, 3 equally spaced colors on the color wheel. High contrast with good harmony. A great combination that always works well. *The quilt 'Who Are You Looking At?' on page 4 makes use of this color scheme.*

Other combinations are split complementary, double complementary, tetradic, square… the list goes on. If you are especially interested in researching more about color combinations one of my favorite books is Joen Wolfrom's 'Color Play: Easy Steps to Imaginative Color in Quilts'(2nd Ed)(C&T Publishing, 2014)

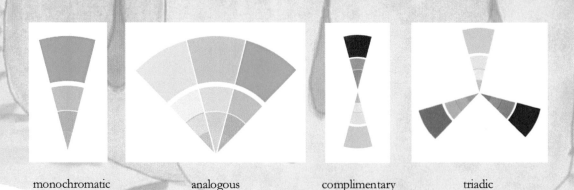

monochromatic   analogous   complimentary   triadic

• Color and Fabric Choices

To select the colors to use for this quilt I took a slightly different approach from normal. Instead of a formal color study (bunny chow is mostly brown!) I thought more about the mood or feeling of the subject. Bunny chow is a hot and spicy dish, so a hot, fiery color palette seemed most appropriate.

By choosing colors from the hot side of the color wheel, reds, oranges, yellows and browns, I knew I would have a quilt that would reflect the spicy character of the subject.

As my hot color palette used fabrics next to each other on the color wheel I had effectively chosen another analogous color scheme. Working with analogous colors is gentle on the eye, so to keep up the spicy energy in the quilt I chose to use vivid fully saturated hues. If I had used lots of pastel tints, tones or shades the quilt would have had a much more muted look, which is certainly not what bunny chow is all about. To add a little 'kick' to the color scheme I introduced an accent of dark green – the compliment to red. This stopped the quilt from being too bland and helped make the chili red pop, adding more visual energy to the overall design. To help with fabric selection later on I used my collection of paint sample cards to create the paint chip palette (below) for the project.

Ask yourself

Which colors does the subject of this quilt call for?

Should it be obvious or quirky?

Paint chips and fabric scraps for Bunny Chow quilt

• Using the Design Toolkit

Design Toolkit© for Quilters -elements
www.clairepassmore.weebly.com

Lines	Shapes	Space	Colors	Textures
			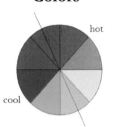	
Thick, thin, straight, curved, zig zag, horizontal, vertical, diagonal, continuous, broken, dotted............. Pay attention to why you drew the lines and what they might be showing	Organic freeform 2D shapes / Geometric 2D shapes. 2 dimensional flat shapes are made from lines which have been joined up They are either geometric or organic	Positive Space / Negative Space. The area around, within or between shapes or parts of shapes Important for perspective. Can be positive or negative	hot / cool. Hues, Shades, Tints, Tones, Values. Color and Value studies help with this element	Texture. Can be physical or visual, real or implied. Makes use of threads, different fabrics and patterns or prints

Horizontal pale blue lines to create the exercise book page & pink vertical line for margin.
Mark these out onto the fabric to create the structure for the page

Cursive handwriting to be created by continuous line quilting
How will I deal with the thread joining the words?

bread

Lots of individual chili pepper motifs – each slightly different
Free cut shapes of bread, saucepan etc.
Letter shapes for title
Appliqué / painted / stenciled / embroidered?????

Arrange the elements on the quilted page in rows to look as if they are from a handwritten recipe book
Margin for small chili motifs, quilted writing on lines spaced in paragraphs, small pictures to illustrate

Hot color scheme to reflect spicy food. Analogous colors; reds, oranges, yellows, browns. Bright and colorful
Shiny silver fabric for saucepan

Use embroidery to embellish the small motifs to give detail, interest and texture
Quilted writing will give lots of relief to the surface

Design Toolkit© for Quilters - principles

(Toolkit for placing design elements)
www.clairepassmore.weebly.com

Harmony	Contrast and Dominance	Rhythm	Balance	Unity
				Overall arrangement of lines, shapes, colors and/or textures complement each other. Nothing appears out of place and there is consistency within the design
Repeated lines, shapes, patterns, colors, motifs or textures. Gives calmness and is easy on the eye. Too much can be boring	Variation of lines, shapes, colors, textures, orientation. Think of opposites, e.g. light and dark. Gives importance, impact & variation	Predictable and organized order of lines, shapes, patterns textures colors or motifs. Can be regular, progressive, alternating or flowing. Helps guide the eye	Elements arranged so that visual weight is balanced; symmetrical, radial, asymmetrical, mosaic, big balanced by many small, or small bright shape balanced by larger dull shape	Grouping and/or repeating elements contributes to unity as does continuing lines, shapes, colors, textures or techniques throughout the design

Create a quilted 'page' from a hand written recipe book, using continuous quilting lines to create rows of text. Scrapbook style? Use the convention of setting out a recipe in steps.... 1, 2, 3......

Repeated motif of single red chilies in vertical rows on sides of quilt. Vary size and shape of each one slightly. Create the border zone

Cursive flowing handwriting in small sections – lay out instruction style will give order and predictability – we are used to reading recipes / instructions top to bottom, left to right

Small images of bread, pans etc. to illustrate the text. Cartoon style. One picture for each step of the instructions

Title letters: at the top– make bold and lighter color to keep lightness at top of quilt

Try title on a curve or letters irregularly placed to keep it informal

Writing and motifs are of equal importance and have their own discrete properties. Red chilies will probably be quite dominant, but text is also dominant, so I think overall it should be balanced

Page layout is already established – on lines. Keep handwritten text in small blocks. As chilies are in a column in the margin, try to echo the column arrangement for the handwriting and other small motifs to give a sense of order

Keep the spaces of each of the different elements defined so as not to become a jumbled mess

Keep the size of the motifs small to be in proportion with the handwriting

Leave a small space around each step of the instructions rather than blending them in together

Don't make it too cramped.

Fuse and appliqué all the motifs onto the quilt

Stitches will form the lines of the 'page'

• Developing the Design

Tip

I keep a box of small ready prepared quilt sandwiches made from offcuts of fabric and batting so that when I need to quickly try out an idea I do not have to stop what I am doing and interrupt my flow.

Looking at the two pages I had made in my sketchbook (see page 107) I used the Design Toolkit once again. Having gone through this process several times by now I found it much quicker and easier to identify the things I wanted to include and the reasons for placing things in certain positions to make best use of them. I liked the idea of making a quilt with a lot of written text as it was something I had never tried before. The nature of free motion quilting lends itself to fluid pattern making, so I thought it would be worth experimenting to see if I would be able to use stitch to make a neat and realistic page of 'written' text. To see whether my free motion skills were up to the task I tried some samples.

Using some small quilt sandwich squares made from cotton batting and quilters weight cotton I experimented with free motion quilting words rather than patterns. I usually have a supply of these squares readymade so that I can try out quilting pattern ideas, thread combinations, tension settings and so on.

Free motion quilted writing sample

As I began to write with the thread I quickly realized that this was, in many ways, easier than the free motion quilting patterns we are used to creating on our quilts. We are so used to writing that we don't even have to think about it so the connection between our hand and brain is almost effortless.

112

Once I had confirmed that I was able to create writing on my quilt I concentrated on the rest of the design. From the Design Toolkit I had already chosen the different elements I would need. The small images of the ingredients and utensils were simple enough to collage out of fabrics and appliqué onto the quilt, so that too did not pose any difficulties. For the background 'page' I again decided to experiment with using different thread colors to suggest the lines and margin. All in all it was a simple quilt design that did not need much further experimentation.

For the quilted 'page' I selected 3 different values of blue; one very light, one light and one medium. I had imagined that it would have been one of the lightest threads that would be most suitable, but as there was only a single line of thread the lightest values were too similar to the white background and almost disappeared. There was not enough contrast with the background fabric, so I was glad I had checked.

This was also the case with the pink thread. It just goes to show the importance of testing out fabric and thread combinations before you start work.

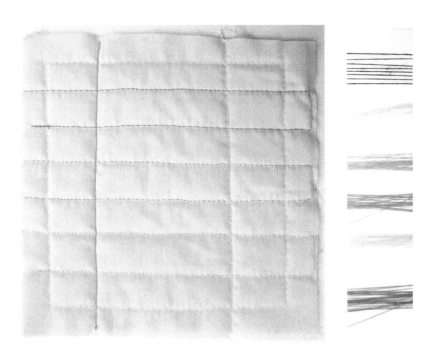

Testing out thread colors for the quilted 'page'

• Pattern Templates

As this quilt was intended to be an interpretation of a page from a child's illustrated recipe book, this somewhat dictated the dimensions of the finished quilt. I chose a rectangle measuring 17" by 25 ½" since the proportions appeared roughly right as a representation of a sheet of paper. I then drew the outlines of the appliqué shapes to fit the space, cut them out and used them as paper patterns. Placing them onto the fabric allowed me to audition them for size and let me experiment with their position. As there were not many appliqué pieces this was an easy way to decide on the final layout.

For the title letters at the top of the page I chose the font called *Impact* and after a little playing about set the font size to 150. I printed out the letters and used them as templates in the same way as for the 'eGoli' quilt I made previously. As you can see, this was a simple quilt so by this stage I was almost ready to begin construction.

Paper pattern pieces for Bunny Chow

Font: *Impact*

Size: *150*

• From Design to Quilt Construction

Because the writing was to be a quilted element I needed to position and stitch the other elements onto the quilt top first. I therefore had to carefully plan the order of my work in a similar way as I had done with 'Sardine Run'. I imagined I was making a collaged page and arranged the lines and little illustrations onto the quilt top before quilting the writing.

To ensure everything ended up in the correct position I marked out the lines on the fabric page with a water soluble pen, using the original sketchbook page as my guide. I measured the fabric, counted the number of lines I wanted for the recipe page and calculated how they should be evenly spaced. This ensured I was able to fuse the appliquéd pieces in the correct positions.

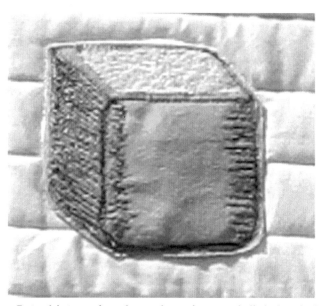

Beige fabric appliqued onto the quilt top, embellished with thread sketching to give the appearance of the loaf of bread

When I was ready to begin construction I gathered together a selection of fabrics from my scrap box which matched the paint chips I identified earlier (see page 109). To make the process of cutting small fiddly shapes easier I applied fusible web to all the scraps before I began. I do not typically do this, as I do not like to commit large pieces of fabric to be used just for fusible appliqué, but as these were already small pieces they were not going to be suitable for anything else, so having them prepared for fusing saved time.

> **Tip**
>
> Check that your water soluble pen / chalk / light erasable pen or other method of marking can be removed from the fabric you are using.
>
> Also check that when the fabric dries there is not a halo or other water mark left.
>
> I speak here from bitter experience!

For the small images of the bread and saucepan I chose pieces of fabric whose color most looked like the things I was trying to represent; pale beige for the bread, a dark rich brown for the sauce and metallic silver for the pan. The silver fabric was particularly troublesome as it frayed very easily, but once it was fused to the web it became much easier to handle. I then used the paper pattern pieces to draw onto the fabrics, cut them out and then fused them to the cream background fabric. Next I sewed carefully around each one with matching thread, adding a little thread sketching detail to permanently attach them to the quilt top.

Layers of organza give a very nice ombre effect

I wanted the large title letters at the top of the quilt to contribute to the 'hot' feeling of the quilt. To make them a little more interesting I thought it would be worth trying to grade their color, from an orange red at the base to a lighter yellow toward the top, rather than just be a solid color. I experimented with some dyed fabric, but the effect was very flat. Whilst searching through my fabric stash for other ideas I remembered the luminosity I achieved using organza on the 'Sardine Run' quilt and decided to replicate that. I found a selection of red, orange and yellow organza scraps; and with a cool iron I carefully fused some applique paper to the back of each. I then layered them onto each other, overlapping each one slightly onto the next. This created a laminated effect with the colors blending well and creating the graduated shading I had imagined. By fusing the layers there was also no problem with the organza fraying, the fabric having become like a soft, flexible plastic. I was so pleased with the result I made a note to use the technique again.

I then used the paper letter templates I had printed out earlier to cut out the letter shapes and fused them in place at the top of the quilt. Rather than placing them in a formal straight line as I had in my sketchbook I tried tilting the letters to make a more informal arrangement. This looked much more dynamic and fun, so I went with that. Finally, with a small zigzag stitch I sewed around the edges of each letter to secure them in place.

• Adding Dimension

To complete the appliqué on the quilt top I added another of my favorite techniques. Rather than having the vibrant red chili peppers along each side of the quilt lying flat on the quilt surface I used machine trapunto to emphasize them with a little more dimension. Once the chili pepper shapes had been cut from the bright red fabric and fused onto the quilt, I added the little green tops and neatly sewed around the outline with a matching red and green thread. For the trapunto I placed a small piece of batting behind each pepper shape, threaded the needle and bobbin with water soluble thread and stitched closely around the outer edge of the chili shapes. I then trimmed away the excess batting as I had done previously with the fish on the 'Sardine Run' quilt. (See page 75)

I liked the way the chili peppers made a border to the rest of the quilt and brought a big hit of color to what would otherwise have been quite a plain quilt. Cover up the chilies and you will see what I mean.

Trapunto effect with a chili pepper shaped appliqué

• Quilting Decisions

Thinking next about the text I wanted to add to the quilt, I needed to decide the most attractive and efficient way to tackle it. I was mindful of the fact that I wanted to minimize the number of starting and finishing tail threads I would have to deal with since I knew I would have to bury each of them into the quilt. From the Design Toolkit I had already decided I wanted a handwritten look with a cursive style so I decided to try out 2 different approaches before I finally made up my mind.

Using very thin (60 wt.) black thread in the needle and bobbin and the free motion darning foot, I first tried free motion quilting words individually, breaking thread between each word. This is the top line of quilting in the sample on the right, and looked very much like conventional writing. Breaking thread each time, however, meant I had lots of starting and finishing threads to deal with.

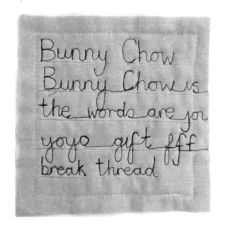

• Design Element: Line as Text

From much experimenting I have found many different ways to successfully incorporate text into my work. Several of the quilts in this series have some sort of writing as part of their design, although I did not set out with this specifically in mind. For each quilt the style and use of the text is a little different as the writing serves a different purpose each time.

Bunny Chow: page 105

The text in this quilt is the main design element. It needed to be clear and legible from a distance so I chose a dark, contrasting thread color and decided to break thread between every word to make it very distinct. Using very thin thread made the text light and easy to read.

Big 5: page 32

The text on this quilt formed the background quilting for the overall design. It tells the story of the 5 most hunted animals in Africa. As it was not a focal point of the quilt I chose a thread color that was similar to the background of the quilt so that it would blend rather than stand out. I also chose to quilt the writing continuously, without breaking thread between each word, mainly for practical reasons. It is a little more difficult to read but is still legible and gives interest and texture to the quilt.

Greetings from the Rainbow Nation: page 46

The text on this quilt is definitely a major focus of the design. Bold capital letters are filled with quilting lines, providing pattern and texture to the design. The words are the greetings exchanged between South Africans on a daily basis in the 11 official languages of the country. As these words are often called out or used as short expressions I wanted the text to be bold and punchy, in contrast to the flowing, cursive style of the previous two quilts where the text provided a narrative.

WARNING : CONTENTS MAY BE HOT !

For the second method I tried running the words into each other without breaking the thread, so that individual words were joined by a continuous line of stitches. This is the second line on the sample square (page 117). When I got to the end of a word I made sure to travel to the baseline and stitch a short line of stitches to form the space before beginning the next word. This was a much quicker and easier method to stitch, but in my opinion made the text much more difficult to read and much less appealing. For that reason I decided to bite the bullet and quilt each word individually, breaking thread each time and burying the threads into the quilt. It took a long time, but overall I think it made for a much more realistic look to the quilted writing.

To make the task of burying the threads back into the quilt easier I made use of an easy thread needle. They can sometimes be a nuisance when sewing, as I sometimes come across a needle that shreds the thread all too easily, but if I buy a packet there are always several 'good' ones in there and I keep them in a special pincushion next to my machine so they are easy to find. To bury a thread simply pull both threads to the top or back of the quilt, pop the thread between

the grooves next to the eye of the needle and stitch the threads back into the quilt. I like to do this as I go along as I hate having to sit for hours sewing ends back into a quilt, and I also do not like having loose threads floating over my work as I inevitably catch them into other stitching and they are then even more troublesome to deal with.

Tip

Keep a quick or easy thread needle next to your machine so you can easily bury starting or finishing threads into the quilt as you work.

Having got to the end of my trials I threaded the machine with the medium blue thread in the needle and bobbin and attached the walking / even feed foot to the machine. This made short work of quilting the lines I had previously marked onto the page and made sure they were straight. For the margin I replaced the blue thread for a medium pink and again stitched the line in place.

Once the lines were done it was then a quick and easy job to free motion quilt the text from my sketchbook page.

• **Border Questions**

Tip

If you have a particularly difficult or complicated pattern to quilt, try drawing it in a fluid movement on a small wipe-off board to get yourself comfortable with the movement. It will give you confidence and help ensure your hand and brain are coordinated before you start on your quilt.

The only parts of the quilt now left unquilted were around the red chili peppers on the left and right borders. As the chilies were fairly small I needed to choose a small scale quilting pattern to complement them. I also wanted the quilting to flatten the border to make the chilies stand proud from the surface even more, so the quilting would need to be quite dense. After some thought I chose a simple stacking pattern that I am very familiar with and feel confident quilting. As I usually do, I made a sketch of the quilting lines so as to confirm my choice and also to get the pattern firmly established in my mind.

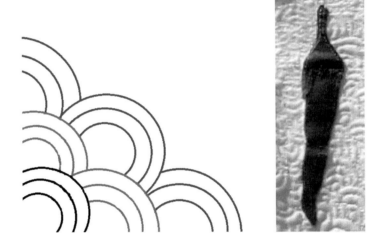

Tiny stacking arch quilt pattern around the chilies forming the border

I threaded the machine with white thread in the needle and bobbin and micro quilted the design around the chilies up to the edge of the quilted page lines, thus forming a border to the quilt, created due to the change in visual texture of the quilting. It is interesting to note that you can create borders for your quilts without adding new strips of fabric just by changing the visual texture with the quilting. The quilt 'Jacaranda City', (page 146) also has borders created in this way.

Before pinning the quilt onto my design wall I stay stitched 1/8" (approx. 4mm) around the edge to neaten it and give a firm finish so that the quilt would not stretch or fray. I then left it there for a few days so I could begin to decide how to bind the quilt.

• Finishing Details

Since this was supposed to be a page from a book I did not think a conventional binding would suit the style of this quilt, but I did have a few ideas in mind:

- satin stitch around the edge (as for the eGoli top quilt)
- turn the edges in to form a knife edge finish
- adding a facing to turn to the back of the quilt
- couching a cord to the edge

I discarded the satin stitch idea as I generally prefer to use this technique on small quilts. The knife edge finish was not going to work well with this quilt as I had already quilted right up to the edges so I would not be able to trim away the batting and turn the front and back fabrics inwards. If I had wanted to use this technique I should have planned for it before I did the quilting.

That left me with either using a facing or couching a cord. I think both would have been equally suitable for this particular quilt, as they both leave a crisp neat edge. In the end I decided to try the cording, as I have never finished a quilt in this way before. Interestingly, it turned out to be very simple indeed, and again I made a note to myself to try the technique on future work.

I used a few yards of what my local supplier calls *rat's tail* – a decorative 2mm satin covered cord.

Before I stitched on the rat's tail I set my machine to a narrow zig-zag stitch (3.5 width on my machine) and sewed once again around the edge of the entire quilt. This gave me a really firm edge to work with for the next stage. I next threaded the machine with invisible thread in the needle and bobbin and put the cording foot onto the machine. Placing the rat's tail right up to the edge of the quilt I zig zag stitched all the way around, pivoting at the corners. When I got back to the start I overlapped the rat's tail by approximately 1/4" to 1/2" (approx. 10mm), trimmed off the excess and continued to zig zag past my original starting place, thus closing the gap and neatly finishing the join. I then added a tiny drop of fray check to the cut ends, although I think this was probably not necessary. The result was very pleasing indeed, and very quick and simple to do. I think it finished this small quilt perfectly.

> **Tip**
>
> I always put my invisible thread onto a thread stand behind my sewing machine so that the thread has room to unwind a little before coming into the machine's mechanism. I find it considerably reduces the amount of tangling and issues with thread tension.

suggestions to try

◇ Try writing with thread – you will be surprised at how easy it is

◇ Practice free motion quilting pattern ideas on wipe off boards or on paper. Try keeping a small sketchbook just for doodled ideas for quilting patterns

◇ Experiment with different ways of binding a quilt instead of your normal method

◇ Make a collection of small quilt 'sandwiches' and keep them within easy reach of your sewing machine, ready to try out new ideas

◇ Spend an hour or two browsing through old magazines and rip out collections of colors. Play with them to form color schemes and stick them into your sketchbook

◇ Enjoy the process

Techniques

Free cut curved piecing

Stenciling

Appliqué

Hand stitching

Free motion quilting

Design Focus

Conveying movement with color and line

'Trance Dance' by Claire Passmore, *18.5" x 40"*

• A trip to the Drakensberg

Just before leaving South Africa for a while, my husband and I decided to take a visit to the Eastern Cape - to the famous Drakensberg Mountains. The whole region is renowned for its beauty and indeed, there was so much inspiration all around it could easily have become overwhelming. If you ever feel you have an inspirational 'block', go to the Drakensberg – you will soon have more ideas than you can cope with!

*My unique
Ardmore bowl*

We rented a small car and drove for miles and miles. We visited the battlefields, which were very moving; we drove the long and winding road to the famous Ardmore ceramic art studio and gallery, met many of the very talented artists and bought a unique souvenir; we listened to the fabulous voices of the Drakensberg Boys Choir and stayed in the most wonderful hotel – Hartford House, alongside Summerhill race horse stud farm. It was a wonderful trip. However my main reason to visit was to see the rock art this region is so famous for, and it is this that my next quilt was based upon.

• South African Rock Art

*The Eland is the
most commonly
depicted animal in
San Rock Art*

Ancient rock paintings and carvings can be found all over Southern Africa, left behind by the indigenous peoples of the region. The mysterious and fascinating images provide a lasting record of the things that were important to their daily life. The majority of the paintings are closely related to the cultural and spiritual lives of these ancient people, and from a very young age I have been fascinated by the imagery, symbols and metaphors that this rock art contains.

If you are interested in finding out more about rock art specifically in South Africa then a good place to start is The Rock Art Research Institute whose website is at www.wits.ac.za/rockart/. There are also many articles and books written by J.D. Lewis-Williams who is widely regarded as an authority on the subject. His book, 'A pocket guide to San rock art' published by Jacana (2011) is especially good if you want a book to take on a field trip. For rock art from around the world there is also an enormous online learning resource from the Bradshaw Foundation; www.bradshawfoundation.com

• Sketchbook Inspiration

Knowing that all of this fabulous inspiration would be around me I went well prepared. Every day I made sure I had my camera and sketchbook with me, so as to capture at first hand many of the things I saw.

Once again the value of a sketchbook as part of my design process was demonstrated with this quilt. As I stared at the amazing scene painted onto the rock I was able to scribble a small and very rough sketch of how I might interpret it as a quilt design. As you can see, the sketch is neither detailed nor very good, but it did capture my thoughts at that moment which I used later on as I settled down to design the quilt. It just goes to show, you don't need to be able to draw a masterpiece to be able to make an art quilt.

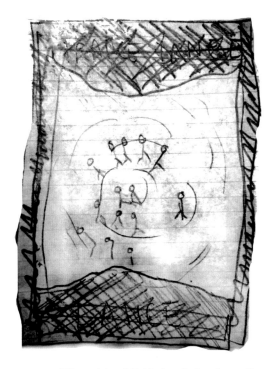

The original field sketch for the quilt

For this quilt I chose a specific piece of rock art that I found particularly interesting. In reality it is only a small image, but it captures one of the most important rituals of the San People – Trance Dance. The scene is full of energy and movement and portrays a ritual where shamans (medicine people) dance in the center as women clap a rhythm and sing special medicine songs. As the dance increases in intensity, the women's clapping and singing combine with the men's persistent dancing to *'cause the potency to boil and to rise up the shamans spines; when it explodes in their heads, they enter a trance and the person is healed.'*

The Trance Dance on a rock wall at Mooi River

• Color Choices

Later that day I painted my interpretation of the scene in my sketchbook with a small set of water colors, whilst the image was still fresh in my mind. To help identify suitable colors I put the photograph I had taken into the MS Paint software on my computer and used the color picker tool to extract a selection of colors from the image.

Color study using MS Paint software

The resulting palette was one of very natural earth colors: ochre, sienna and umber, which given the subject matter, I suppose should not be a surprise as these natural pigments have been used since prehistoric times.

Once I had painted the background and the figures in the dance I experimented with adding the swirling lines in the background in an attempt to emphasize the movement of the men around the Shaman in the original painting.

Left: My sketchbook interpretation of the original rock art image

• **Using the Design Toolkit**

Design Toolkit© for Quilters - elements
www.clairepassmore.weebly.com

Lines	Shapes	Space	Colors	Textures
	 Organic freeform 2D shapes · Geometric 2D shapes	 Positive Space · Negative Space	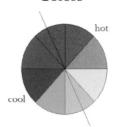 hot · cool	 Texture
Thick, thin, straight, curved, zig zag, horizontal, vertical, diagonal, continuous, broken, dotted............	2 dimensional flat shapes are made from lines which have been joined up They are either geometric or organic	The area around, within or between shapes or parts of shapes Important for perspective. Can be positive or negative	Hues, Shades, Tints, Tones, Values Color and Value studies help with this element	Can be physical or visual, real or implied Makes use of threads, different fabrics and patterns or prints
Pay attention to why you drew the lines and what they might be showing				

Lots of short curved lines around the dancers to show the circular movement of the dance Create with seams / very thinly pieced strips or applique / fabric paint / stitch

Horizontal wavy lines representing the cracks and relief in the rock onto which the picture is painted; choose fabric carefully and try to use mottled fabrics to replicate the texture

Swirling curved lines give the feeling of the circular movement of the dance

Human figures in various poses; applique or fabric paint (screen print or stencil?)
Try to replicate the figures and their poses as accurately as possible

The point of interest is the Shaman and his patient in the center; the rest of the scene surrounds that fairly compactly; the remaining space is the textured rock background

Color study provided lots of rich earthy colors and grays in values from light to dark.
The rock surface / background has a generally light value to make sure the darker figures will show up clearly.

The rock surface is very rough and mottled; the fabric will need to have a very broken color, with lots of visual texture; batik or unevenly dyed fabric

Design Toolkit© for Quilters - principles
(Toolkit for placing design elements)
www.clairepassmore.weebly.com

Harmony	Contrast and Dominance	Rhythm	Balance	Unity
				Overall arrangement of lines, shapes, colors and/or textures complement each other. Nothing appears out of place and there is consistency within the design
Repeated lines, shapes, patterns, colors, motifs or textures. Gives calmness and is easy on the eye. Too much can be boring	Variation of lines, shapes, colors, textures, orientation. Think of opposites, e.g. light and dark. Gives importance, impact & variation	Predictable and organized order of lines, shapes, patterns textures colors or motifs. Can be, regular progressive, alternating or flowing. Helps guide the eye	Elements arranged so that visual weight is balanced; symmetrical, radial, asymmetrical, mosaic, big balanced by many small, or small bright shape balanced by larger dull shape	Grouping and/or repeating elements contributes to unity as does continuing lines, shapes, colors, textures or techniques throughout the design.

The human figures/motifs are continually repeated; the extra lines can emphasize movement; repeat them in different ways for variety; make more subtle than the obvious figures

In the original there are 2 similar values of umber for the figures, painted without detail or shading
The figures are relatively dark in color when compared to the lighter sandy-beige background; the different poses and sizes of the figures will be important to stop the image being too repetitive
The background will need to be very mottled to give the impression of being painted on the roughly textured rock surface; create a hand dyed fabric with a very light gray base with streaks of darker grays and shades of umber and ochre

The repeated human figures in the circular arrangement are fundamental to this design; everything about trance dance concerns rhythm – the clapping of the women, the movement of the men and the chanting of the shaman
This needs to come across strongly in the design; lots of carefully arranged repetition of elements will be needed – seams /appliqué / paint / stitch
I like the idea of adding the extra lines around the dancers to reinforce the circular movement and to add to the rhythm of the design

The dance is circular in form and the figures are presented in a closely formed radial design with a central focal point; putting these in the center of the quilt with other elements echoing this circular arrangement is important so as to not change the balance of the design; aim for a swirling effect

The focus of the quilt is going to be contained in the central image; supporting elements will create the swirl; the palette is very limited to natural earth colors and grays; unity should not be an issue

• Developing the Design

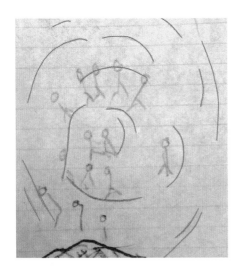

Several weeks later, when I was ready to work on the design, I pulled out my sketchbooks and photographs and began to think about how I was going to interpret the images in fabric using the Design Toolkit.

I knew I wanted to recreate a fairly realistic interpretation of the original art, but I also wanted to capture the sense of the circular movement of the figures in the scene. I looked back at the small hastily scribbled picture I had drawn and noticed I had used small curved lines to suggest the rotational movement of the dance and so decided to make them part of the design.

My outline drawing of the Trance Dance

130

• Design Element: Line

Line plays such an important part in quilt design as there are lines everywhere on our quilts: seams, quilting stitches, the edges of appliqued pieces and surface embellishment all make lines on our quilts. These lines define shapes and areas, give physical and visual texture to our work and guide our eyes around a quilt. The *quality* of the lines can also be varied to have different effects (line quality is a range of attributes which describe a line: for example: thin, thick, solid, broken, rough, smooth etc).

With this quilt I have taken advantage of using as many different ways to create lines as I could think of to help contribute to the impression of swirling movement. I used the patchwork technique of free curved piecing to create the quilt background. The curved seams created the foundation to the rest of the lines I placed on top. Next, I used fabric paints and pastels to draw and paint soft curved lines onto the fabric surface. On top of that I appliqued more defined curved strips of fabric to create a layer of slightly thicker lines. Finally I hand stitched and machine quilted broken curved lines with thread to give a mass of directional lines all curving around the central image of the dancers.

Think carefully about the lines on your quilts and how you can use them to contribute to the overall effect you are looking to achieve.

Since the dancing figures from the scene would be the obvious focal point, that element needed no further thought, except for the method I was going to use to add them to the quilt.

That left the area remaining around the figures. In the original rock art, the painting was positioned on an outer edge of rock wall and as I did not want to frame the piece with a conventional rectangular border (I did not think it would be in keeping) so I experimented with adding a dark, jagged section above and below the main image to further suggest a rocky wall. I penciled that in to my sketchbook image to see how it looked, and I thought it might work. I was not completely sure, but I felt I would be able to trial the idea whilst the quilt top was being constructed.

With those ideas in mind I drew and redrew the whole scene until I was completely satisfied with the way it looked and then enlarged it using PosteRazor.

Pattern for the Trance Dance quilt

• Testing Ideas

As you have seen from my earlier quilts, my design process often involves experimenting with different techniques and ideas before I make my final design decisions. Not only does it help me choose the methods I use for each quilt, but occasionally I end up with surprising results which take the work off in a completely different direction. I know it adds to the overall time a quilt can take to make, but for me it is part of my process, and significantly enhances the final quilt design. I enjoy this part of the process very much.

As this quilt was to be an interpretation of an original piece of rock art I had the idea that I wanted to paint the scene onto the quilt surface. Whilst I liked the idea of freely painting onto the fabric, just as the original artist would have done, I was a little nervous of my ability to render a good interpretation without making mistakes and ruining the whole piece. For that reason I decided to try the idea of making a stencil and applying the paint that way.

Using freezer paper, I drew one of the figures from the scene and cut out the shape with a small craft knife. I ironed the paper onto a piece of fabric and tried several different media to color the fabric the stencil revealed. I tried soft pastels, Markal oil sticks, Derwent inktense blocks and fabric paint, all applied with stiff brushes or my fingers. All gave excellent results, but the effect I liked most for this quilt was a burnt umber fabric paint as that seemed to be the most true to the original.

Once I had made my final decision to use the stencil I was able to trace the pattern I had drawn onto a large sheet of freezer paper and cut out the appropriate parts with the craft knife. Making such a big stencil was a large investment of time, but the result was good, and I knew that if I was careful with it I could use it again to produce further work.

Trialling the stencil for the Trance dance figures. Here I used soft pastel, fixed with clear fabric extender

For the background I had already decided that I was going to use sweeping, curved lines to add to the feeling of movement in the scene. To see which methods would be most suitable I tested adding lines onto a small piece of fabric in several ways:

- curved seams
- thin strips of fabric appliqued to the background fabric
- hand and machine stitched lines
- liquid fabric paint and oil stick paint.

It was interesting to note the different qualities of each type of mark. The seam lines were subtle, but allowed me to change the color and value of fabrics on either side of the line, and also added curved shapes to the background. The soft pastel gave a gentle, slightly fuzzy line, which when smudged with my finger blended a little into the background. I liked that very much. The strips of fabric gave more 'thickness' to the lines and when I added hand stitching on top of them they contributed more visual weight and texture to the overall design. Happily I liked the effect of all the techniques, so I chose to use them all.

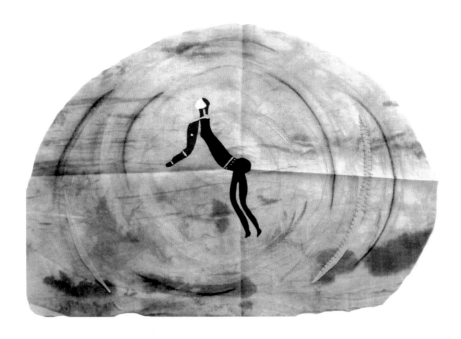

Experimenting with different techniques to add swirling lines of movement

• Fabric Choices

For the ochre painted figures to show up well I decided that the pieced background fabrics ought to be quite light to ensure a good contrast in value. When I referred to the photographs I had taken I saw the background rock was a similar color to the figures I would be stenciling on later. I thought this might make the quilt too monochromatic and bland, so I took the decision to alter the color of the background a little to very light grays and peachy-rust pastel tints. Since I was portraying a rocky surface I thought mottled, streaky effects would be good. Learning from my experiences whilst making the 'eGoli' quilt earlier in the series I knew how I wanted to dye the fabrics to obtain these effects.

I mixed up the dyes as normal and used 'Method 1' (see p159) and scrunched up as much soda ash soaked fabric as I could into small plastic cups. I then poured over the dyes, most of which were very dilute to ensure light values. Using a pipette I added very small amounts of more concentrated dyes here and there to give streaks and spots of random color and then left them to soak for a few hours in a warm place. After rinsing and drying they were ready to use.

Procion MX Dyes

Better black
New black
Black
Camel
Bronze
Brazil nut
Golden yellow
Midnight blue
Fuchsia

• From Design to Quilt Construction

To piece the curved seams for the background I had two choices:

- to carefully cut out the pattern pieces, transfer them to my fabric and then stitch them together. This would give a very precise background that matched my original drawing and would look very nice. However that would be a lot of work, and I really did not need that degree of accuracy.

- to take a more improvised approach and use a rotary cutter to cut curved fabric pieces suggested by the pattern. It is a simple and very quick method of piecing curves, but does rather go against what traditional patchwork has taught us in terms of precision and accuracy. However, do not be afraid! It is a simple technique to master.

First, I took two pieces of fabric (A and B) that were a little larger than the patches I finally wanted. I laid fabric A right side up on the cutting mat and cut a gentle curve the full length of the fabric with the rotary cutter. Next, I placed fabric B onto the mat, also right side up. I made sure that the curved cut edge of fabric A overlapped the new piece of fabric along the complete length and then used it as a template to rotary cut fabric B to match. I followed the curve as exactly as I could, so that both pieces fitted together like jigsaw puzzle pieces, as you can see in the photograph below.

I then repeated the process with fabrics B and C

Tip

It is possible to piece fairly tight curves using this technique, but to start with keep it simple and cut gentle curves.

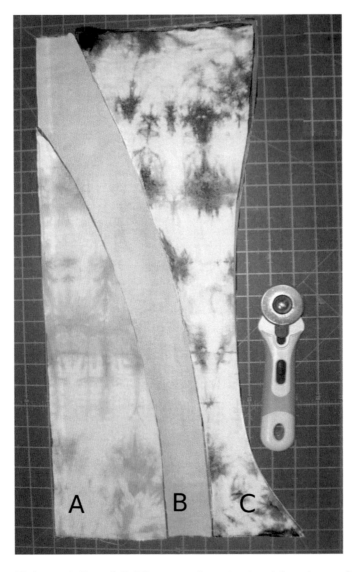

Fabrics A, B and C. The curves fit each other (almost) exactly

To join the pieces I set the machine to sew a straight stitch, but shortened the stitch length just a little. I placed the fabrics right sides together and matched up the first inch or so. The fabrics did not match up as with sewing conventional straight seams– but at this stage it does not matter. (If you are familiar with setting a sleeve into a shirt you will be used to this.)

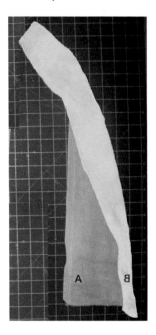

Using a scant ¼ inch seam (or ⅛ if possible) I stitched in short bursts, just a few stitches at a time. By stopping and starting often I was able to gently move the top piece of fabric so the curved edge lined up with the bottom piece. I then sewed a few more stitches. I did not pin the pieces together, but matched the edges as I sewed. In my experience pinning takes up lots of time and is more trouble than it is worth when stitching gentle curves. It really depends on how sharp the curves are, how tight the weave of the fabric is and how comfortable you are with 'winging it'!

Once I reached the end of the seam I had the two pieces of fabric joined with the top fabric (B) laying rather puffily on the bottom piece (A).

Here you can see fabric A (right side up) and fabric B (wrong side) stitched together. It is worth noting that the top fabric did not end at the same place as the bottom fabric. Look and you will see the bottom of fabric B extends beyond the edge of fabric A.

This is quite normal with this technique and is why I started with fabric that was slightly larger than I needed.

If you like to pin your seams then use sharp thin pins. Start at one end and ease the fabrics together, matching the cut curved edges. Try not to pull or distort the fabrics as you handle them otherwise the seams will become very bumpy.

Do not worry if the fabric lengths do not match at the end.

Finally, I opened out the fabrics and pressed with lots of steam allowing the seam to sit whichever way the fabric wanted to go. By sewing a scant seam it was not necessary to clip it – but with really tight curves do whatever you need to do to get it all to lie flat. I then trimmed the edges with my rotary cutter and ruler so that I had an even bottom edge.

I took a log cabin type approach to my piecing – starting with a central piece of fabric that was rather melon shaped, and then added a piece to the curved right hand side. After pressing I cut a curve on the left side and added another piece of fabric. I carried on in that fashion until I had a large enough panel for the background.

I mixed a selection of very mottled grayish-green fabrics with gray and beige to allow the curved sections to be distinct from each other.

For one final addition to the feeling of movement I pieced the darkest gray section on the lower right so that it appeared to run out of the edge of background. Because it is different from the rest of the curves in color and shape it attracts the eye and provides an entry / exit point to the circular pattern.

The completed pieced background

• Adding Stencils

Once the background was finished I was then able to get back to the stencil I had drawn and cut out from the freezer paper. Being careful not to tear the paper I carefully positioned the stencil, shiny side down, onto the pieced background, making sure the central figures were positioned in the middle of the fabric. With a fairly hot iron I gently pressed the paper, allowing the shiny backing of the freezer paper to temporarily fuse itself to the fabric. With it fixed in this way the stencil could not move, which would cause the image to become smudged or misshapen. It also helped ensure no excess paint could seep under the edges of the stencil, blurring the nice crisp edges I wanted.

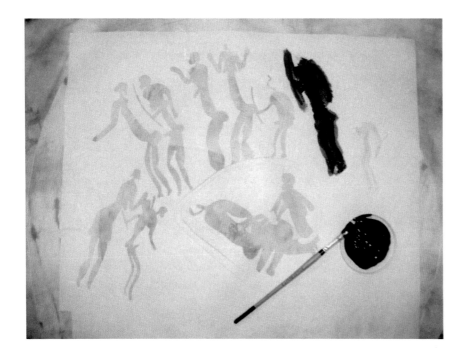

Painting the Trance Dance scene using a freezer paper stencil

I then applied the burnt umber fabric paint with a small flat paintbrush, carefully brushing from the edge of the paper towards the center of each figure. I was careful not to saturate the fabric as I did not want any paint to bleed under the edges of the stencil. I took my time and tried to apply the paint as evenly as possible.

Once the paint was dry I very gently peeled the freezer paper away from the fabric, and saw the beginnings of the Trance Dance scene appear. Referring back to the photograph I had taken, I added the small details my stencil had not been able to include.

With all that done I just needed to set the fabric paints with a very hot iron to make sure they were permanently fixed. Make sure to follow the manufacturer's instructions for your product.

Adding detail to the painted figures after the stencil was removed

• Adding Detail

Small strips of fabric added to the background

As the main image was now painted onto the quilt I was able to turn my attention to developing the sense of the movement that I was so keen to capture.

The seam lines were the beginning of this, but I wanted much more rotation. I pinned the quilt to my design wall, then prepared a small selection of fabrics by fusing appliqué paper to the back. I cut lots of thin, curved strips from the fabrics and positioned them onto the quilt as I worked. I tried to ensure there was a variety of contrast between the color and value of the strip and the background fabric so as to make the strips visible, but not too obtrusive.

I played about with the color and position of the strips until I was happy with the effect and then left the arrangement for a few days to make sure I liked what I had done.

Over that time I decided that although I liked the effect, the strips alone were a little too obvious and not really blending in as much as I wanted. Rather than remove them completely I wondered whether perhaps what was needed was something more, rather than less. Taking the plunge, I got out the soft pastels that I had experimented with earlier when trying out ideas for the stencil. I remembered that I liked the way they blurred and blended with the fabric. Although very messy to work with I had also discovered that when the lines were painted over with clear textile medium this not only fixed the color but also controlled the dustiness of the pastels.

Just to be certain that the effect would be suitable I took the small experimental piece of fabric I had created earlier. Using a selection of grays, tans, browns and whites from the box of pastels I drew sweeping curves onto the fabric, between the fused strips. The weave of the fabric made the pastel line soft and slightly fuzzy in appearance and as I rubbed it with my finger I was able to blend it even more. This was exactly the effect I was looking for, so I then began work on the quilt, adding lots of lines in and around the strips I had fused on earlier.

Using soft pastels to add lines to the quilt

I was careful not to make a mess with the pastels on other areas of the quilt, since they made quite a lot of intensely pigmented dust. After I had washed my hands thoroughly I was able to handle the quilt to shake and remove this excess unwanted dust before painting over the new lines with textile medium to fix them.

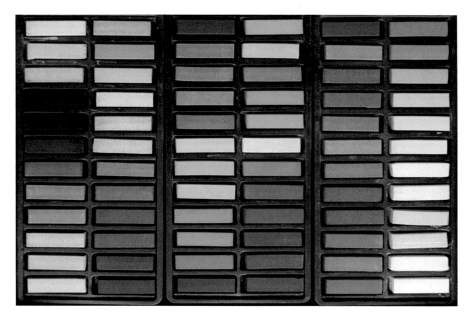

Soft pastels used for adding pigment to the fabric

• Border Decisions

Tip

To help you make decisions, take photos of different layouts, color choices or other options as you work. You can then flick through them and more easily decide which options you like best.

I had made some tentative plans for the borders of the quilt at the start of my design, but I was not 100% certain whether they would work or not. For me, sometimes the only way forward is to wait and see – and this was one of those times. Now the quilt top was looking the way I wanted, I began to focus on how to deal with the borders.

On my design wall I began to try out different options; I pulled some dark gray fabric from my selection and draped it across the top of the quilt. By pinning it in different positions I was able to step back and see how it looked. I also took a few photographs of different arrangements so I was able to flip through them and compare the different ideas. I really like to use my camera in this way as it helps isolate the quilt from its surroundings and also allows easy comparisons.

Very quickly I was able to see that I did like the dark fabric at the top and bottom of the quilt – but not at the sides as that took me back to the frame idea that I was trying to avoid.

With this decided I cut the fabric and appliquéd it using the traditional needle-turn technique to the quilt top.

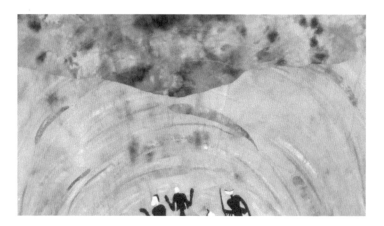

Gray fabric for the top and bottom 'borders' of the quilt

• Quilting Decisions

As I mentioned earlier, quilting lines also play a part in the overall design of a quilt. Still thinking about how I could emphasize the movement of the dance I chose to make the quilting lines curve around the group, echoing the small strips and pastel lines already on the quilt top. Constantly repeating the use of line had a harmonizing effect on the overall design, but by creating those lines in different ways I was able to add interest and variety to what would otherwise have been quite a simple quilt.

The thread color blended so well I have altered the photograph so it can be seen!

Choosing the right thread color was also important to the overall design. For a subtle effect, blending the lines into the background rather than having them as a focus, I chose a thread that would not shout too loudly - a charcoal colored rayon, with a little sheen. This gave the textural movement I was looking for, but not any particular interest. To give just a little more definition to some of the lines I added some texture by using a thicker hand quilting thread and hand stitched them. This gave just a little more definition to the lines and gave direction to the eye of the viewer, moving their gaze around the quilt.

Tip

Think of what you want the quilting lines to achieve; do you want them to be subtle and gently add to the texture of the quilt? If so echo shapes with a similar color.

Or

Do you want to make a statement and add some bold new lines? If so contrast the shape of the lines and perhaps use a contrasting thread.

• **Not quite finished**

To be sure the quilt was finished I pinned the quilt to my design wall and left it hang for a few days. As pleased as I was with it, it still did not look 'finished'. I liked the movement I had achieved with the different types of line and I liked the unusual top and bottom borders – but it was lacking something. I tried experimenting with different colored bindings, but I was still not satisfied. In the end I gave up my resolve not to put a framing border around the piece and tried out a plain dark gray strip and identically colored binding around the four sides. The moment I added the borders everything fell into place and I knew it was finished. So much for my determination *not* to have a frame!

suggestions to try

⬧ Try a color study using the computer to pull colors from a picture

⬧ Experiment with creating freezer paper stencils to create shapes on your quilts instead of appliqué

⬧ Try using pastels (and any other artist materials you may have) on fabric and fix with fabric extender for a different effect

⬧ Think about different ways to make lines and shapes on a quilt top – be creative with the materials you already have

⬧ Try different ways to create quilt backgrounds – such as piecing, strip piecing or curved piecing then build your quilt on top of that

⬧ Experiment and see what you can come up with!

⬧ Enjoy the process

• Final thoughts

Now that you have seen the processes I use to design and create my own original art quilts I hope you will have begun to formulate some of your own ideas and strategies for creating your own original work.

There is no magic recipe that I follow, but there is a basic structure that I begin with.

Sketchbooks are the root of my work – a place to gather and explore ideas.

The Design Toolkit gives me a framework which helps me to sort those ideas, identifying what to use in the quilt and how it can be brought together as a pleasing composition.

Experiments with materials and techniques help me to develop those ideas and allow me the time and space to see what might work.

Eventually there comes a time when I have enough well thought through ideas to create the design. However, I believe it is important to say that whilst you can have a great idea and plan for a quilt, there is no real way to know how things will turn out until the quilt is made. For me, making art quilts is an evolving process; I begin with an idea, which I grow into a plan. As I make the quilt all sorts of further ideas occur to me and I make changes along the way. Sometimes ideas work, and sometimes they don't. Have the confidence to deviate from your plans should you need or want to. Just because you planned something doesn't mean you have to stick to it. I learned that with the 'Trance Dance' quilt.

The other thing I have learned is not to rush – when I am not sure about something, I stop and think, sometimes for weeks! Unless you have a deadline to meet, why pressure yourself and spoil the enjoyment?

I hope that reading about my journey with these quilts has been helpful, and that you have begun to try out some of the suggestions I have mentioned. Remember to do what works for you – don't be put off by what others say or do. I am a firm believer in being an individual and trusting my own judgment. For me there is no right or wrong way to do something. If something you try works – great! If it doesn't, then try to figure out why, and try again. But most importantly of all.....

enjoy the process.

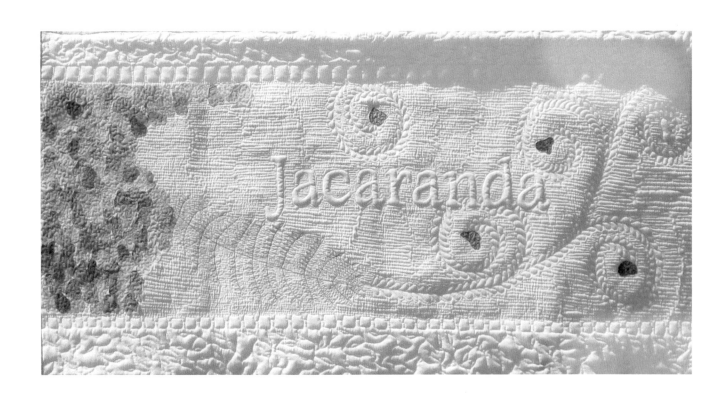

'Jacaranda City' by Claire Passmore, *39 ½" x 19"*

Part 3

Dyeing your own fabric is not only fun to do, but also gives you *almost* complete control over the originality of your work. I say 'almost' in a positive sense, as you never quite know what you will get until you rinse and dry your fabrics – but I am never disappointed after a dyeing session, as the unique fabrics created are always beautiful.

To dye fabric yourself you need a minimal amount of equipment and a few chemicals - and you will be delighted to know that none of it is expensive! So, read through this basic 'how to', and then see if you feel you would like to try to create your own hand dyed fabrics. It really is worth the small extra effort.

Obviously there are sensible precautions to be taken when handling dyes and chemicals, particularly powders. Procion MX dyes are declared non-toxic by the manufacturer, but they can aggravate allergies or pre-existing conditions, so follow these simple guidelines to ensure you dye safely.

- Avoid inhaling powder or dust: wear a face mask when handling and measuring out all dry powders

- Protect your clothes and skin from splashes – this stuff stains! Take a simple 'non-contact' approach.

- Do not use tools or equipment that you also use for food – use recycled containers and dedicated measuring cups etc.

- Keep your working area clean. Use a drop cloth to protect surfaces and have cloths ready for wiping up spills.

- Store all chemicals in clearly labelled, sealed containers out of the reach of children and animals.

- Dispose of all unused dye liquids safely. Dilute and pour down the drain.

• Which fabrics can I dye?

When you use Procion MX type dyes you will achieve the very best results when you use 100% cotton, rayon, linen, ramie, hemp, bamboo, jute, modal, Lyocell or Tencel fabric, which has been pre-washed to remove any surface treatments. Alternatively you can purchase 'Prepared For Dyeing' fabric, more commonly known as 'PFD', which has already been stripped of any surface treatments which may interfere with the dyeing process. Some say it is wise to pre-wash even this fabric, but I usually do not bother.

It is possible to get reasonable results with some polycotton fabrics (at least 50% cotton), but this is much less reliable and you will always end up with pale colors. For that reason, the recipes and methods I give here have been written for use with 100% cotton fabric.

• What do I need?

To keep things simple, I have made 2 shopping lists: one for chemicals and one for equipment. Items with an asterisk* are optional. As long as you have the basics from the top of the lists, you will have everything you need for basic dyeing.

Chemicals

Procion MX type dyes
Regular non-iodized salt
Soda Ash (more correctly called sodium carbonate or 'pH plus' from pool shops)

*Urea
*Sodium Alginate
*Synthrapol detergent

Fiber reactive dyes such as Procion MX type dyes are permanent, reliable and very easy to use. They are also inexpensive and safe, unlike many other types of dye on the market.

These dyes are available as long lasting powders in over 100 different colors. By mixing them with water you create liquid dyes which are simple to use and can be stored for up to about a week. Technically it is possible to create all the colors you need by just mixing the 3 basic colors of *lemon yellow, fuchsia and turquoise* so these are good colors to start with. For convenience, however, you may like to try some of the blended colors that are available. Suppliers have color charts which give a good indication of the colors you can achieve.

A list of suppliers is on page 171.

How it works

One of the reasons these dyes are so easy to use is that you can dye at room temperature. During the dyeing process the dye molecules physically bond to the fibers of the fabric you are dyeing. To ensure the dye molecules bond properly, you need 3 things:

1. to leave enough time for the dye to penetrate and bond.
2. to increase the pH of the dye bath to around 10.5. By adding sodium carbonate (soda ash) the perfect conditions are created for the dye to permanently bond to the fabric.
3. to have a temperature between 95°F and 105°F (35°C and 41°C), although temperatures as low as 70°F (21°C) can work given longer soaking time.

Soda Ash (sodium carbonate) is well known as a household product. As a degreaser and water softener it is sold as washing soda, but due to its chemical composition is not the best choice for dyeing. Sodium carbonate is also used as a swimming pool chemical, where it is referred to as 'soda ash' or 'pH plus'. When purchased from dye suppliers it is known as 'soda ash dye fixer'. I find the most economical way to buy it is from the swimming pool shop. Just be sure to purchase sodium carbonate, NOT sodium bicarbonate, which will not raise the pH enough to fix the dye to the fabric.

Soda ash is a white powder that mixes well with warm water. Whilst not a particularly dangerous chemical, it can cause skin and respiratory irritation, so make sure to wear gloves whilst handling it and wear a mask or respirator until it is mixed with water.

Salt. Any ordinary salt will work, but small grains dissolve more quickly. It is said that non iodized salt is preferred, but I have not found any noticeable difference in results when I have used iodized salt instead. It is also said that a chemical known as Glauber's Salt (sodium sulfate) is better when working with turquoise dyes, but again, I have seen no noticeable improvements when using this product over ordinary salt.

*Urea is another white chemical that can assist dye in certain situations. It attracts water, thus stopping fabric drying as quickly as it normally would and so giving more time for the dye to penetrate the fibers. It can also help certain dyes to dissolve better, so allowing you to get more concentrated dyes. Too much however, can have the opposite effect. As with the other chemicals, avoid inhaling the dust and excessive contact with skin.

*Sodium Alginate is made from the seaweed known as kelp. It is commonly used in the food and makeup business, and is completely non-toxic. Sodium alginate is a natural thickener and can be mixed to create a thick or thin gel, depending on the amount of liquid you add. Use it to make dyes a little more like paint or to reduce the amount of natural spreading of the dye. It can also be used if you decide to explore stamping, stenciling or screen printing with dye.

Equipment

Pre-washed or PFD fabric
Measuring spoon set
Measuring cup set
Disposable gloves
Dust mask or respirator
Apron
Plastic drop sheet
Bucket(s)
Old cloths

Recycled items such as:
Yoghurt pots /glass jars
Plastic bottles
Plastic tubs or trays
Stirring sticks

*cheap plastic pipettes
*small squirt bottles
*small spray bottles
*sponges
*old food blender or whisk

As you can see from the picture to the right, much of what you need to dye can be collected from the recycling box. Old plastic or glass food containers or recycled resealable food bags can be very useful as they come in a variety of sizes. I keep all of my containers in an old paint bucket, which also comes in handy for soaking or rinsing fabrics.

For measuring out the chemicals a set of very small measuring spoons is useful, but not really necessary. When I mix dyes I am not too precise when I measure. You can be very detailed and measure dye powders etc. by weight if you wish to get consistent results between batches – but I have never needed that much fabric all of the same color or value. For me, variety is what I am looking for, so a more casual approach to measuring suits my needs.

Because the dyeing process requires a few hours of your time and some space to set out lots of pots and so on, I usually plan to set aside a morning or afternoon for the process. I tend to mix the dyes I am going to use at the beginning of a dyeing session and try to use them all up that day. You can, however, store mixed dyes for about a week (some say longer) in tightly sealed and labelled bottles.

*Synthrapol is a type of liquid detergent that some say is particularly good at removing excess dye when you come to rinsing at the end of the process. This excess dye can transfer to other parts of the fabric and cause unwanted results, known as back staining. Personally I have not found it to be any better or worse than ordinary dish washing liquid. However, as it is not expensive or difficult to obtain you may want to try it out. Just remember to use a very small amount – a teaspoon or less, as it is ultra-frothy!

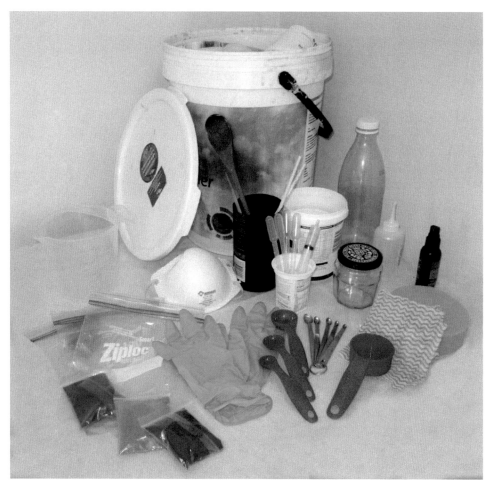

Clockwise from the top: large paint bucket, recycled bottles, tubs and jars, sponge, cloth, measuring cups and spoons, pipettes, gloves, dye powders, recycled resealable bags, measuring jug, dust mask, wooden spoon and stirrers

154

• Mixing the chemicals

Once you have the equipment ready you need to prepare your work space and mix the chemicals. From experience I find the following setup works well:

- **Soda Ash** solution. Put on your gloves and mask. Measure 4 pints (approx. 2 liters) of hand hot water into a bucket and sprinkle over ½ cup of soda ash. Stir gently until it is fully dissolved. As soon as the powder is mixed with the water you can remove your mask. You can mix this in large quantities if you wish as it stores well.

  Note: I usually mix up quite a lot and keep it in a lidded bucket or recycled bottles. Make sure to label it clearly and keep it out of the reach of children and animals.

  > Soda Ash Recipe
  >
  > ½ cup soda ash
  >
  > 4 pints (approx. 2 liters) water

- **Urea Solution**. Also referred to as 'chemical water' by some people. Put on your gloves and mask. Measure 2 pints (approx. 1 liter) of warm water into a bucket and sprinkle over ½ to ¾ of a cup of urea. Stir until fully dissolved. As soon as the granules are mixed with the water you can remove your mask. You can mix this in large quantities if you wish as it stores well. Make sure to label it clearly and keep it out of the reach of children and animals.

  Note: Urea is not essential to dyeing, but can help you to obtain more vibrant results. It is particularly good to use when you want longer soaking times or you want to stop the dye drying out quickly, such as when you paint with thickened dye.

  > Urea Solution Recipe
  >
  > ½ to ¾ cup urea
  >
  > 2 pints (approx. 1 liter) water

- **Thickening Paste**. Although not strictly necessary, put on your gloves. Measure 1 cup (approx. 250ml) of urea solution into a large container. Gradually sprinkle over 1 tablespoon of the sodium alginate, whisking as you go. The seaweed tends to clump, so try to take your time and keep whisking. Leave it to stand for around an hour and stir again. I make my paste quite thick and slacken it as necessary. You can also mix it in a blender, but good practice states that you should not use equipment for dye chemicals that you also use for food preparation – so an old blender dedicated to this purpose would be required. Store in a sealed and labelled jar in the fridge for up to one month.

  > Thickening Paste Recipe
  >
  > 1 cup urea solution
  >
  > 1 tablespoon sodium alginate

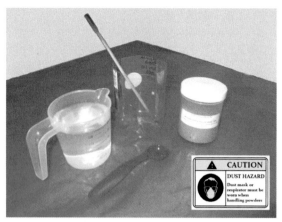

1. 1 cup of warm water, mixing pot and stirrer, dye and measuring spoon

2. Measure 1 teaspoon of dye powder into the mixing pot

3. Add a little water to moisten the powder and mix to make a paste

4. Add the remaining water and stir very well until all powder is mixed

5. Add around half a cup of salt and stir until dissolved

6. Pour into a bottle for safe storage Close tightly and label

• Mixing the dyes

Before you start to mix the dyes, fill a bucket with water and place it close by so that you can drop dirty spoons, pots etc. straight in. It helps to keep things clean and speeds up the cleaning process at the end.

- Set out the number of dye powders you are going to mix. I usually start with the basic 4: lemon yellow, fuchsia, turquoise and black. Gather together a pot and a plastic spoon / stirrer for each dye.

- Put on your gloves and mask/respirator. Measure out 1 cup (around 250ml) of clean lukewarm water and place it to the side. Measure 1 teaspoon of dye powder into a pot and immediately drop the dirty spoon straight into the bucket of water. Take a teaspoon or two from the lukewarm water you put to the side and add to the powder, then mix to make a paste. I find wetting the dye powder a little at this stage helps it to mix more easily.

- Top up the pot with the remaining lukewarm water and stir until the powder has completely disappeared. This can take a few minutes, so be patient. You can remove the mask now if you wish. Keep stirring until all traces of lumps are gone. If you really have problems you can filter the dye through a nylon stocking, but it is best to try and get rid of the stubborn tiny lumps by stirring. I find that reds can be particularly troublesome.

- Add about half a cup of salt to the dye and stir until dissolved. The quantity is not so critical, but it is said that the salt helps to 'push' the dye into the fibers. (I have forgotten to put it in on odd occasions and I can't say I have noticed much difference.)

Once mixed, put the dye to one side where it will not get knocked over, or pour the concentrate into a bottle and screw the cap down tightly until you are ready to use it.

Dye Recipe

1 teaspoon dye powder

1 cup lukewarm water in total

½ cup salt

This makes a fairly dark, intense dye concentrate. Add more water for paler colors and more dye powder for even deeper colors.

• 3 ways to apply the dye

Once you have prepared the dye and the chemicals you are ready for the magic to begin. Depending on the type of result you are aiming for there are 3 methods I use:

Method 1	Method 2	Method 3
Soak the fabric in soda ash solution first and *then* add the dye	Add the dye first and *then* add the soda ash solution later	Mix the soda ash solution and dye together. Often used in conjunction with urea or dye thickener
Use this when you want to try to reduce mingling of dye colors or you want a patchy, streaky or tie-dyed effect	Use this when you want different dyes to mingle and blend	Use this when you want to paint, stamp, stencil or screen print with dye or when you want more control over where the dye goes

Why is the timing of adding the soda ash so important?

Once the soda ash is introduced, the clock starts ticking as the dye starts to deteriorate. The soda ash forces the available dye to immediately begin the process of bonding to the fabric fibers, and the dye now only has a few hours of 'life' before the reaction stops working.

If you leave time for the dye to soak into the fabric fibers before you add the soda ash the dyes have time to mingle and merge before they fix to the fabric. If you add the soda ash before the dye the reaction begins immediately, and the dyes do not have as much time to merge and mingle. It also means that if the dye has not completely wetted and soaked into every fiber, patchy, mottled or even undyed areas will remain.

Method 1: Pre-Soaking the fabric

To prepare the fabric you need only soak it in soda ash solution for around 20 minutes, but I often leave mine in the bucket overnight. When you are ready, squeeze out the excess water with your gloved hands and either use the fabric straight away (damp), or leave it to dry naturally if you want to start with dry fabric. You are now ready to apply the dye.

Tip

Do not iron fabric that has been soaked in soda ash – it scorches very quickly.

These are the sort of mottled or streaked results you can achieve when you use fabric that has been pre-soaked in soda ash

Method 2: Starting with untreated fabric

If you are starting with fabric that is prepared for dyeing (PFD) you can go straight to adding the dye. You can start with dry fabric, or you can moisten it a little with a mist of water if you want the dyes to begin running into each other immediately.

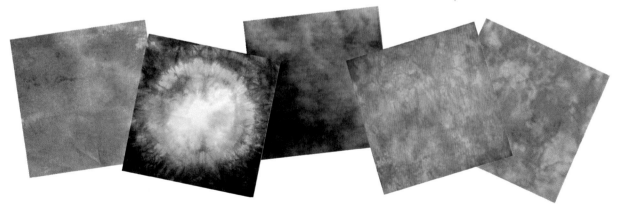

And these are the more blended results you can expect if you add the soda ash later

159

Applying the dye for methods 1 and 2

Fabric, bags, pots and squirty pipettes

Bag method: crumple the fabric into the bag, and then add dye onto the fabric

Squeeze the bag gently to mix the dye just a little
More squeezing = more mixing

Pot method: squish the fabric tightly into the pot.
Put some dye in the bottom if you wish

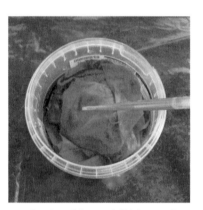

Squirt, drip or dribble on dye
Use one or more colors and add a little urea solution if you want to dilute certain areas

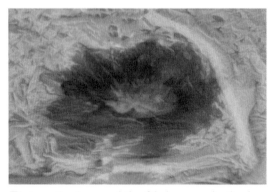

Flat method: spread the fabric on a plastic sheet and apply dye with brushes, sponges or pipettes.
Blend colors with urea solution

Applying the dye for methods 1 and 2

- Scrunch the fabric into a very small pot or plastic bag – as tightly as you can. The more creases and folds you have, the more uneven the result will be.

- Dribble, squirt or drip your chosen dye color(s) onto the fabric, being sure to get some dye down towards the bottom. Try not to over saturate the fabric. You can even try squeezing a little dye into the center of the squished fabric. Use as many or few colors as you wish, but do think about how colors mix to avoid a very sludgy brown mess if you choose to use several colors. There are no hard and fast rules, and the best way to learn is to dye lots of small pieces of fabric (fat quarters or smaller) to see what happens. Remember that you can dilute the dyes with water to get lighter values.

- Once you have added the dye, use a gloved hand to poke or squeeze the fabric around a little to make sure you don't have too many blank patches.

- Alternatively you can lay the fabric out on a large sheet of plastic or on a large flat tray, depending on the size of your fabric. It can be flat, twisted, pleated, gently crumpled…. however you choose. You can then add the dye by brushing, spaying, squirting, dripping, sponging or any other technique you can think of.

Twisted fabric can have dye painted or squirted on it to give a nice streaked effect

Loosely crumpled fabric can have dye squirted over in a more controlled way

Batching the dyes for methods 1 and 2

Once the dye has been applied to the fabric and the soda ash is also present it is necessary to allow enough time for the dye to bond to the fibers in the fabric. This part of the process if often called 'batching'. The most important thing to remember during this part of the process is to keep the fabric warm (minimum 70°F /21°C) and moist for a minimum of 1 hour. If you wish to leave it longer then no harm will come to the fabric, and it can even be helpful in reducing back staining.

Batching for method 1: Because the soda ash is already soaked into the fabric, as soon as the dye is added all you need to do is leave it to soak. The optimum temperature is between 95°F and 105°F (35°C and 41°C) and if you think the fabric may dry out during this time cover it with plastic or plastic food wrap.

Batching for method 2: You need to leave the dyes to mingle and merge for up to an hour *before* you add the soda ash; the longer you wait the more the dye will migrate around the fabric, but too long and the colors may merge completely and blend into one. When you like the way the dyes have mingled it is time to add the soda ash fixer. Pour it slowly and carefully over the fabric until it is completely saturated. It is only when the soda ash has been added that the bonding process begins. Once you have added the soda ash solution leave the fabric in a warm place for at least an hour, just like for 'method 1'.

Batching the fabrics

Rinsing the dyed fabrics for methods 1 and 2

Once you have batched the fabric you need to rinse it to remove any excess unbonded dye. You need to take care over this as it is still possible for some of that excess dye to attach itself to the fabric in places where you do not want it. This is known as back staining, and it can ruin your hard work up to this point.

A good point to remember is that once mixed with soda ash the dye not only starts to bond with the fibers, but it also begins to deteriorate. You can take advantage of this fact by leaving the fabric to batch for such a long time that the dye becomes completely deteriorated by the time you come to rinse. This will mean that back staining will be reduced or avoided completely, as there is no more 'life' left in the unbonded dye to spoil your work.

Using very hot water (140°F / 60°C) in the final rinse can also help, as high temperatures also contribute to the deterioration of the dye.

Wearing gloves, remove the fabric from its container and either immerse it in a large bucket full of water or hold it under a running tap. This does, however use a lot of water, so choose your method carefully depending on how large your fabric is. The aim is to get as much of the excess dye out of the fabric as quickly as possible to stop any remaining unbonded dye from attaching itself.

Rinse the fabric until the water you squeeze out is reasonably clear. If you are using the bucket method of rinsing you will need to change the water a few times to get to this point.

You can now fill a bucket with water as hot as your gloved hands can manage (extra thick dishwashing gloves are good) and add half a teaspoon of Synthrapol or a good squirt of dish washing liquid. Immerse the fabric into the soapy water and massage with your hands to encourage the last of the excess dye out of the fabric. If you have a very large piece of fabric you may prefer to do this in your washing machine – choose a hot cycle.

Once you are completely satisfied that no more dye is running out of the fabric you can put it into your washing machine and wash it on a normal cycle. Once dry it is ready to use.

Method 3: Adding soda ash and dye at the same time

This method is most often used when you want to use thickened dye which will stay exactly where you put it, with little if any bleeding or blending with the colors around it. It is the method I used to dye the graduated blue background fabric for 'Sardine Run'. The drawback with this method is that the clock starts ticking as soon as the dyes are made up, since you mix the dye powder with soda ash powder from the start. This means you will need to work a little more quickly when preparing the dyes and then get them onto the fabric reasonably quickly.

It is my preferred method of applying dye if I am going to paint, stamp, stencil or screen print with dye, or when I want to have more control over how the dyes merge with each other. You will need to experiment with the thickness of the paste you prefer for each technique.

Before you start, try to estimate how much thickened dye you will need. If you are unsure, start with about half a cup and see whether you think that looks likely to be enough. You will not be able to store this if you make too much – and disliking waste I try to make as much as I think I will need.

- Put on your gloves and mask and measure out the estimated amount of thickening paste into a tub. For each whole cup of paste add ½ a teaspoon of soda ash and *up to* 1 tablespoon of dye powder. The amount of dye powder you need will depend on how dark you want the dye to be. Mix the paste thoroughly until everything is well blended. You now have a few hours to use this dye.

- Test the intensity of the dye color on a piece of scrap fabric or kitchen towel and adjust accordingly, adding more paste if it is too dark, or more dye and soda ash if it is too light. If you need to thin the paste use a little urea solution.

- Spread the fabric on a large sheet of plastic. The fabric or the plastic can be smooth or crumpled, depending on the effect you want to achieve. Experimenting with small pieces of fabric is the best way to become familiar with the variety of results you can achieve. Apply the thickened dye using brushes, sponges, stamps, syringes, squeeze bottles, piping bags, stencils or screen prints, in fact any method you can think of!

Batching and rinsing

Once the thickened dye has been applied to the fabric the batching and rinsing process is exactly the same as for 'method 1'. To avoid back staining you may want to batch overnight or even longer and you may have to work a little harder to rinse the fabric since the thickening paste clings somewhat to the fabric. Nevertheless, the extra work is worth it as the results you can achieve are fabulous.

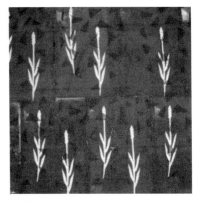

Screen printing with a freezer paper mask and thickened dye. Triangles were then sponge printed over the top with blue thickened dye

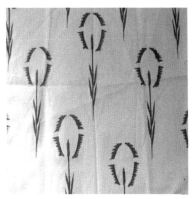

Screen print using a freezer paper stencil and thickened dye on gray PFD cotton fabric

Cookie cutter stamp used with thickened dye on white PFD cotton fabric

Safe disposal of used dyes

Once you have finished dyeing you need to dispose of the dyes responsibly. Pour the dye liquids down the drain and flush with lots of clean water. Any left-over thickened dye needs to be diluted with water until it is thin enough not to block the drain. The manufacturer safety sheets state that the dyes are non-toxic and will not damage your septic tank.

I do not consider myself a fussy quilter and am happy to use whatever materials I have available. As I travel a lot I often have to make do with what I can carry, borrow or afford in any one place. One of the more important implications of such wanderings concerns measurement. Metric or imperial? Only having an inch ruler when you need one in centimeters can be a real nuisance. Perhaps that is one of the reasons I seldom make quilts that need critical measurements any more! Nevertheless, I do have a large collection of rulers and cutting mats scattered all over the world, but they never seem to be in the right place at the right time.

There are, however, a few items that I really do feel lost without. They are not essential by any means – but I feel comfortable when I have them. Fortunately they are neither large, nor expensive, so I have a set everywhere I go.

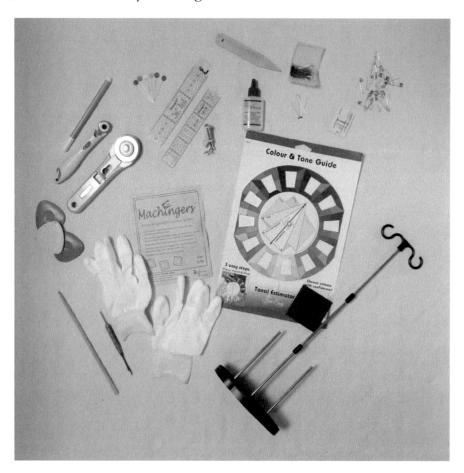

Clockwise from the top: wooden iron, extra fine pins, safety pins, topstitch sewing machine needles, color wheel, thread stand, quilters' gloves, an old blunt dart, chopstick, tailors chalk, large and small rotary cutters, water soluble pen, flat head pins, quilters rulers, free motion darning foot, fray check.

• Useful Computer Software

There is a variety of software I find particularly useful in helping develop my ideas and designs, and like any tool we all have our favorites. There are many different types of software that do similar things and some are better than others. Some can be expensive whilst others are generously provided for free. Whilst I do not personally endorse any particular software, this is what I most often use:

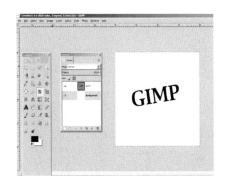

GIMP: Image manipulation software that can be freely downloaded from the internet. Absolutely no payment is required. I use it to alter and manipulate images to create my patterns, to experiment with color and value and to try different layout ideas for my designs. It takes time to learn how to use it, as it is complex software, but personally speaking, I find the time I have invested in learning how to use the software has repaid itself many times over. There are literally thousands of free tutorials on the internet to help you learn and a great online support network if you need help.

Electric Quilt: I bought Electric Quilt, perhaps more commonly known as EQ7, several years ago. It is great software and with it you can very easily design block based quilts in a relatively short time. It is great for trying out color schemes, and you can even design with the very fabric you are going to use. It is fairly expensive, but if you make a lot of block based quilts then I think it is worth it. Personally I almost never use it now, but it is a useful tool and on the occasion I do want to use traditional quilt blocks in a design, (such as when I made 'Storm @ Cape Point', page 2) then I find it a great time saver.

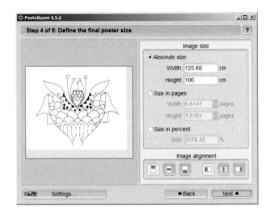

PosteRazor: This easy to use software enlarges or reduces the size of an image – just like a photocopier. It is my go-to software when I am ready to create the full size pattern for a quilt. I particularly like this software as it makes resizing images at home quick and easy. Once you have an image on your computer you simply open it with the software and then resize it, by percentage, number of pages or by dimensions measured in imperial or metric units. One feature I particularly like is that I can see the results before I print them, so I waste far less paper.

After you have made your size selection you save the resized image as a PDF file which can be printed out onto any sized paper. You then tape or glue the sheets together to create the whole resized image.

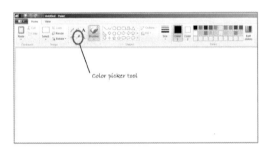

MS Paint: As a PC owner this software automatically came with the computer. It is a basic piece of software that allows you to draw or 'paint' on the screen. I like it because it is simple and straightforward and has a color picker tool

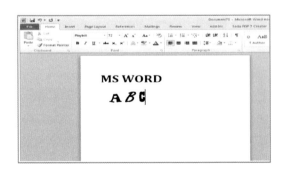

MS Word: As with MS Paint, MS Word came with my PC. It is the word processing software with which many people are familiar. I use it for creating letter stencils or templates.

• Useful websites

These are some useful websites that I also make use of:

Color palette generator (see page 27)

Go to the website, upload a picture of your choice and a color palette will be automatically generated from the colors in the image.

www.cssdrive.com/imagepalette/

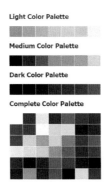

National Geographic

An enormous source of inspirational images

www.nationalgeographic.com

Wikimedia Commons

A fabulous source of open source images. These images are able to be reused and/or shared with few or no restrictions. Each image has a description of the conditions under which it may be reused.

www.commons.wikimedia.org

Bradshaw Foundation

A non-profit making organization dedicated to the study, recording and protection of rock art with a vast learning resource concerning rock art from around the world.

www.bradshawfoundation.com

Rock Art Research Institute
University of the Witwatersrand

The Rock Art Research Institute

Part of the University of Witwatersrand; 25 years of continuous research have made South African Rock Art amongst the best understood in the world.

www.wits.ac.za/rockart/

• **Procion MX type Dyes**

These are old, well established and trusted dyes that are commonly used to create beautiful hand dyed fabrics. They belong to a family of dyes known as *fiber reactive dyes* and are known to be stable and have been declared non-toxic by the manufacturer. Also known as *dichlorotriazine dyes* or *cold reactive dyes*, they work at room temperature which is very practical for home dyeing. Being very fine powders, Procion MX type dyes can aggravate allergies or pre-existing conditions, so follow the manufacturer's guidelines to ensure you dye safely.

They were originally manufactured by ICI in UK but the patent on the dyes has expired and many manufacturers around the world now make them. Hence I refer to them as Procion MX *type* dyes. (Note: in Australia and New Zealand it is sometimes easier to purchase Drimarene K dyes which are similar, but require slightly warmer temperatures to get them to fix.)

They can be used with a wide variety of techniques such as batik and other resist methods, shibori, tie-dye and other tied methods, screen printing, painting or spraying to create beautiful, unique fabrics.

Fiber reactive dyes work with cellulose fibers such as cotton, rayon, linen, ramie, hemp, bamboo, jute, coir, sisal, banana and pineapple fiber, reeds, modal, Lyocell and Tencel.

• Supplies

DYES AND CHEMICALS

BATIK OETORO (Australia)
+61 (0)2 4943 8808
www.dyeman.com

Kraftkolour (Australia)
+61 (0)1300 720 493
www.kraftkolour.net.au

G&S Dye (Canada)
1-800-596-0550
www.gsdye.com/

Creative Craft Supplies (NZ)
+64 (0) 4 4771052
www.creativecraftsupplies.co.nz

Tillia dyes and fabrics (NZ)
++64 (0) 3 214 7964
www.tillia.co.nz

Art Van Go (UK)
+44 (0)1438 814946
www.artvango.co.uk

Handprinted Ltd (UK)
+44 (0) 1243 696789
www.handprinted.net

Kemtex (UK)
+44 (0) 1257 230220
www.kemtex.co.uk

Dick Blick (USA)
1-800-828-4548
www.dickblick.com

Dharma trading Co (USA)
1-800-542-5227
www.dharmatrading.com

Pro chemical and Dye (USA)
1-800-228-9393
www.prochemicalanddye.com

THREAD

Sewing Selections (Australia)
+61 (0)2 6884 0403
sewingselections.com.au

Cansew inc. (Canada)
1-800-361-7722
www.cansew.com

Sewing supplies Ltd (New Zealand)
+64 (0) 9 579 0401
www.sewingsupplies.co.nz

ACA Threads (South Africa)
+27 (0) 21 981 1133
www.acathreads.co.za

Barnyarns (UK)
+ 44 (0) 1765 690069
www.barnyarns.co.uk

Superior threads (USA)
1-800-499-1777
www.superiorthreads.com

PDF FABRIC

Trend-Tex Fabrics inc (Canada)
1-800-667-9448
www.trendtexfabrics.com

Whaleys (UK)
www.whaleys-bradford.ltd.uk/
+44 (0) 1274 5767218

Miller Textiles (South Africa)
+27 (0)21-531-3300
www.millartextiles.co.za

Dharma trading Co (USA)
1-800-542-5227
www.dharmatrading.com

Empress Mills (UK)
+44 (0)1282 863181
www.empressmills.co.uk/

MY FAVORITE QUILT SHOPS

Midsomer Quilting (UK)
+44 (0)1761 239333
www.midsomerq.com

Stitch 'n Stuff (South Africa)
+27 (0)21 674 4059
www.stitchnstuff.co.za

'Forced Removal' by Claire Passmore, 47" x 19 ½" (page II)

'Where Two Oceans Meet' by Claire Passmore, 13" x 31" (page 48)

McDowell, Ruth B Ruth B. McDowell's Piecing Workshop, C&T Publishing, 2007

Wolfram, J Color Play (2nd Ed), C&T Publishing, 2014

Lewis Williams, J D San Rock Art (Pocket History Guides), Jacana Media, 2011

About the author

Claire Passmore lives in the rolling green chalkland of Wiltshire in the UK and Cape Town, on the beautiful south western tip of Africa. She started stitching in 2005 and since then barely a day passes when she does not create something with fabric and thread.

Claire's love of teaching and quilting has resulted in the creation of this book which she hopes will inspire you to create your own original work.

Design Toolkit© for Quilters - elements

www.clairepassmore.weebly.com

Lines	Shapes	Space	Colors	Textures
			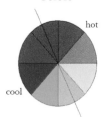	
	Organic freeform 2D shapes Geometric 2D shapes	Positive Space Negative Space	cool hot	Texture
Thick, thin, straight, curved, zig zag, horizontal, vertical, diagonal, continuous, broken, dotted.............	2 dimensional flat shapes are made from lines which have been joined up	The area around, within or between shapes or parts of shapes	Hues, Shades, Tints, Tones, Values	Can be physical or visual, real or implied
Pay attention to why you drew the lines and what they might be showing	They are either geometric or organic.	Important for perspective Can be positive or negative	Color and Value studies help with this element	Makes use of threads, different fabrics and patterns or print

Please feel free to copy this for your own use

Design Toolkit© for Quilters - principles
(Toolkit for placing design elements)
www.clairepassmore.weebly.com

Harmony	Contrast and Dominance	Rhythm	Balance	Unity
				Overall arrangement of lines, shapes, colors and/or textures complement each other. Nothing appears out of place and there is consistency within the design. Grouping and/or repeating elements contributes to unity as does continuing lines, shapes, colors, textures or techniques throughout the design
Repeated lines, shapes, patterns, colors, motifs or textures. Gives a calmness and is easy on the eye. Too much can be boring	Variation of lines, shapes, colors, textures, orientation. Think of opposites, e.g. light and dark. Gives importance, impact & variation	Predictable and organized order of lines, shapes, patterns textures colors or motifs. Can be regular, progressive, alternating or flowing. Helps guide the eye	Elements arranged so that visual weight is balanced; symmetrical, radial, asymmetrical, mosaic, big balanced by many small, or small bright shape balanced by larger dull shape	

175

www.clairepassmore.weebly.com

• A

Angelina fibers 76

appliqué 72,115,117

art materials

  fabric paints 76,97,139

  oil sticks 133

  soft pastels 9,141

  watercolors 16,28,63

  sketchbooks...9,10

  soluble pencils 133

  soluble pen... 15

• B

balance 35,**88**

batting 74

binding 102,103,144

borders 70,142

• C

color **108**,127

  analogous 63, 85,108,

  chips 85,109

  complimentary 108

  definitions 22,63

  hints & tips, 31

  monochromatic 108

  picker tool 27

  saturation 109

  selection 16,30,32,127

  study 21,**26**,27,28,29,
  85,127

  value study 14,23,24

  vocabulary 29,33

  wheel 36,109,166

contrast 36

couching 121

curved piecing 136

• D

depth 69,73

Design Toolkit **38,39,
49,57-58,86-87,110-
111,128-129,174-175**

dominance 36,**88**

dye 66,170

  application 158

  batching 162,165

  chemicals...150

  disposal 165

  equipment 152,153

  Method 1 92,159,161

  Method 2 159,161

  Method 3 166

  recipes 155,157,164

  safety 149

  shopping lists 150,152

  supplies 135,171

  thickened dye 164

Index

• E

elements of design   34,39

  line   16,19,35,36,38,41, 42,44, **118,131**,134,140

EQ7   41,44, 167

• F

Fabric

  PFD   150,172

  Hand dyed   148,154

finishing   102,121

focal point   24,36,97,132

free motion quilting   75, 77,93,98,112,120

fused appliqué   72,115

fusible web   67,68,97,115 116

fusing   72

• G

GIMP   7,27,30,41,44,167

grayscale   23,73

glue, spray   76,92

• H

harmony   36,**61**

• L

line   16,19,35,36,38,41, 42,44, **118,131**,134,140

• M

machine needlelace   94,95

machine trapunto   73,117

materials

  oilsticks   133

  paint   76,97,139

  pastels   9,141

motifs   18,19,42,59,115

• N

needles

  topstitch   74,93

  easy thread   119

needlelace   94,95

net   69,77

• O

organza   69,116

• P

paint   76,97,139

paint chips   15

pastels   9,141

patchwork   19

patterns   14,41,42,90,132, 160

photographs   7,12,15,19 21,44,142

pH plus   151

piecing   136

PosteRazor   41,44,168

Principles of design   35,40

  balance   16,35,42

  contrast   36

  dominance   35,36,38

  harmony   36,38

  rhythm   37

  unity   37,38,42

Procion MX   170

• Q

quilts   II, IX, XII, 2,4,32,46,48,52,53,81,105, 123,146

quilt blocks   19,

• R

raw edge applique 72,115, 117

resist, wax   66

resizing   41

rhythm   37,129

rinsing   163,165

• S

safety   149

salt   151

satin stitch, 96,102

saturation, color 31

sequins   78

shape   21,

sketchbook ideas   10,13, 15,16,17,18, 19

• S

sketchbook pages   8,10,11, 12,13,14,15,16,17,18,19,24 28,55,82,84,107,125,126

sketchbook sizes   10

soda ash   151

sodium alginate 152

sodium carbonate 151

soluble pen   115

soluble thread   74

soy wax   66

stenciling   138,139

• T

Techniques

  Binding   9

  curved piecing   136,137

  free motion quilting   20

  machine trapunto   73,117

  needlelace 94,95

  stenciling   133

  fused appliqué   47

  thread sketching   115

• T

templates   90,114

texture   16,,74,75,115,143

themes   5

thread   113,143,171

thread stand   93,166

tjanting   66

Toolkit **38,39,49,57- 58,86-87,110-111,128- 129,174-175**

topstitch needle   74,93

tracing   98,101

trapunto   74,117

• U

unity   88,**99**,101

urea   152,155

• V

value   21,24,26,28,33,36, **64**

  grayscale   28

  value study   **23**,24,25,2

Made in the USA
Las Vegas, NV
08 February 2024

85483787R00114